Market Relations

Market
Relations

James Butler

PITMAN
PUBLISHING

London · Hong Kong · Johannesburg · Melbourne
Singapore · Washington DC

For Stefania De Vanna

PITMAN PUBLISHING
128 Long Acre, London WC2E 9AN
Tel: +44 (0)171 447 2000
Fax: +44 (0)171 240 5771

A Division of Pearson Professional Limited

First published in Great Britain in 1996

© Pearson Professional 1996

The right of James Butler to be identified as Author
of this Work has been asserted by him in accordance
with the Copyright, Designs and Patents Act 1988.

ISBN 0273 62203 X

British Library Cataloguing in Publication Data
A CIP catalogue record for this book can be obtained from the British Library

10 9 8 7 6 5 4 3 2 1

Typeset by M Rules, London
Printed and bound in Great Britain by Clays Ltd, St Ives plc

The Publishers' policy is to use paper manufactured from sustainable forests.

Contents

Contents

Employee relations • Local community relations • Green marketing • Implications of green marketing • *Self-assessment test questions* • *Group activity*

5 Marketing for services and non-profit organisations

Service quality • Marketing and non-profit organisations • Defining customers for non-profit organisations • The marketing mix for non-profit organisations • Marketing control for non-profit organisations • *Self-assessment test questions* • *Group activity*

6 Social responsibilities

Consumerism • Societal marketing • Cause marketing • Ethical issues in marketing • Product quality and standards • Controls on marketing • *Self-assessment test questions* • *Group activity*

7 Competitive position

Market size • Market share • The product life-cycle • The Boston Consulting Group matrix • The General Electric business screen • Products and brands • Identifying competitors • Competitor objectives and strategies • Competitor strengths and weaknesses • Predicting competitor behaviour • Industry structure and profitability • The experience curve effect • Profit impact of marketing strategies (PIMS) • Marketing as warfare • *Self-assessment test questions* • *Research activity*

8 Types of data

Sources of internal secondary data • Customer information • Product information • Sources of external secondary data • Computers and data analysis • Marketing research • Marketing research process • The scope of marketing research • *Self-assessment test questions* • *Research activity*

9 Survey planning

Observational research • Experimentation • Motivational research • Survey research • Sampling • Selection of a sample size • Postal surveys • Telephone interviews • Personal interviews •

Group discussions • Consumer panels • Retail audits • Designing
questionnaires • Measures • Uses of company databases •
Self-assessment test questions • *Research activity*

Contents

◆ Preface

This book has been written for students studying the BTEC core module 'Market Relations'. The chapter contents of the book closely follow BTEC's guidelines for this module.

My principal aim in the writing of this text has been to provide students with an up-to-date introduction to the required topics of study. I have tried to steer a middle course between burdening the student with too much theory and skimming over sometimes difficult concepts.

Marketing is a dynamic and changing business discipline and I have indicated in the text some of these areas of change – hence the addition to Chapter 4 of the section on green marketing.

I hope that students will find this book a stimulating introduction to a subject of great importance.

JTF Butler
March 1996

Acknowledgements

The author would like to thank Kara Regan and Pradeep Jethi of Pitman Publishing for their advice and assistance during the writing of this book.

Marketing orientation

After reading this chapter you should be able to:

◆ **Explain what is meant by an exchange relationship**

◆ **Distinguish between the production orientation and the sales orientation**

◆ **Describe what is meant by the marketing orientation**

◆ **Outline a marketing department's principal functions**

◆ **Describe the different ways a marketing department can be organised.**

Our first intention in this chapter is to arrive at a definition of marketing. To do that, we are going to look first at what is meant by trade, and then at some of the most important historical developments in recent trade practice and theory.

Trade occurs when people exchange one item of value in return for another. In primitive societies we can imagine how individuals might exchange animal skins for food, or simple crop produce for weapons. The people engaged in such transactions are said to be participating in an 'exchange relationship'.

We should consider for a moment the characteristics of an exchange relationship. The first thing to notice is that there must be two, or more, parties for exchange to take place. Second, each party must have something of value to bring to the exchange. Finally, the exchange must be voluntary, with one party being free to accept or reject the offer of the other party.

As societies become more complex, three important trade developments occur: the use of money, the rise of specialist skills, and the emergence of merchants or 'middlemen'.

The development of money increases the complexity of exchange relationships, but it also brings with it considerable advantages. Once a unit of currency has been accepted, it becomes possible to plan the exchange process. Where previously one item was given in exchange for another, individuals can now sell something one day, and keep the money obtained until they wish to buy something in the future.

Another consequence of the development of money is that the relative value of products can be quickly increased or decreased, as circumstances change. An outbreak of cattle disease, for example, might mean that the price of cattle will increase. In the same way, a good harvest might mean that the price of some crops will decrease.

Even in comparatively simple societies some individuals acquire specialist skills, such as house-building, baking or tool-making. This concentration on specialist skills, which is known as the division of labour, adds greatly to a society's prosperity. It makes more sense for an individual to perfect one skill than to attempt to make everything which may be needed. When there are many specialist producers in a society, there is a huge increase in the amount of trade done.

Merchants or 'middlemen' begin to emerge when small, independent producers start to make their products in anticipation of demand. We can imagine, for example, a candle-maker deciding to increase production just before the onset of winter, when demand for artificial lights increases. Merchants buy products in large quantities and store them until they are required, as in the case of the candle-maker's products. Merchants also distribute the products they have bought throughout a wide area, thus helping to spread prosperity geographically.

So far we have given a brief, general description of how trade develops, and of the exchange relationship on which it is based. Now it is time to look at more specific, recent developments in western societies, in order to trace the development of marketing itself.

 ## The origins of marketing

The Industrial Revolution in Britain began in the 1750s. In its first phase the population of the country increased dramatically, and at the same time, improvements in agricultural production provided jobs and food for the rising population. Road- and canal-building followed, as did the first generation of factories, driven by steam power. Living standards during this early phase of the Industrial Revolution rose markedly, and the demand for goods increased as a result.

During the Victorian era, Britain became an urban, industrial society. The railway system was begun, and cities such as Birmingham and Manchester grew up around the new manufacturing industries.

Industrialisation also took place in America. From the 1850s until the 1920s the greatest problem for American business was to make enough products to satisfy demand. Managers concentrated on increasing levels of production as a first priority, in the belief that customers would buy standard, mass-produced products if the price was low enough. Within businesses themselves, the production department predominated over other departments. The Ford motor-car factory epitomised this 'production orientation'. It was cheaper for the company to make cars in one colour only, and Henry Ford informed his customers that they could have 'any color as long as it's black'.

By the late 1920s the problem of making enough products to satisfy demand had been largely solved in America. Factories were now working at greatly enhanced levels of productive efficiency. The supply of goods was outstripping demand, as factories competed against one another. Managers now concentrated on increasing sales levels as a first priority, in the belief that selling, even if high pressure tactics were used, was the key to business success. This 'sales orientation' of American business led to the use of many 'hard sell' practices which have since become illegal.

After World War 2, American production continued to outstrip demand, and managers began to realise that company profitability depended on understanding and responding to consumers' needs, and making products which would satisfy these. Thus, the 'sales orientation' gave way to the 'marketing orientation'. Managers concentrated on the identification of customers' needs as a first step towards making products designed to satisfy those customers.

We have now reached the first part of our definition of marketing. Marketing is about the satisfaction of customers' needs. Before adding further to the definition, it is important to clarify some marketing terminology.

 ## Some key concepts

Needs, wants and demands

Marketing is about the satisfaction of customers' needs, wants and demands. It is therefore important that we consider what is meant by these terms:

Needs can be defined as the influences which drive human behaviour. Biological needs are for the things necessary to physical survival, such as food, clothing and shelter. Psychological needs include the need for security, gratification and prestige. Human needs are general to all people, irrespective of culture, and they exist before the existence of business organisations. Water is an example of a human need.

Wants can be defined as the wish for specific needs-satisfiers. Wants are culture-specific, and they exist as a result of business organisations. When thirst (a need) is translated into the desire for a particular drink, such as Coca-Cola, it has become a want.

Demands can be defined as human wants for specific needs-satisfiers, which are supported by the ability and willingness to purchase them. A thirsty person who wants to drink Coca-Cola and has the money to pay for it, has a demand for the drink.

An exchange transaction occurs when two or more people satisfy their needs by agreeing to exchange something of value in return for payment. The following kinds of exchange transactions take place in modern societies:

◆ commercial exchanges – when goods or services are exchanged for money

◆ employment exchanges – when work is exchanged for money

◆ civil exchanges – when government services are exchanged for taxation payments.

When economists use the term **market** they usually mean both buyers and sellers. In the marketing world, however, market usually refers to buyers only, and the term **industry** is used to indicate sellers. From a marketing perspective, therefore, the Coca-Cola market is made up of Coca-Cola purchasers.

The *production orientation* has been defined by Peter Doyle as follows:

> **Production orientation: the management view that success is achieved through producing goods of optimum quality and cost, and that, therefore, the major task of management is to pursue improved production and distribution efficiency.**

We have seen how the production orientation resulted from the pressure to meet rising levels of demand, and how it made use of mass-production techniques to achieve this objective. From an historical point of view, the production orientation can be seen as successful in that it did make new products widely available. It should be remembered, however, that its success occurred in a period when there was a shortage of mass-produced goods. As soon as customers were presented with greater product choices, the weaknesses of this approach to business were revealed.

From a marketing perspective, the production orientation has significant disadvantages. First, it is an approach to business that is company-centred rather than customer-centred. It concentrates on productive capacity and price rather than on the satisfaction of customers' needs. Second, it relies on an economic environment in which demand is greater than supply.

The *sales orientation* has been defined by Peter Doyle as follows:

> **Sales orientation: the management view that effective selling and promotion are the keys to success.**

We have seen how the sales orientation resulted from the failure of the production orientation, once the supply of goods had outstripped demand for them. The sales orientation encourages businesses to engage in aggressive selling techniques which frequently alienate potential customers.

From a marketing perspective, the sales orientation also has significant disadvantages. Like the production orientation, it is company-centred rather than customer-centred. It concentrates on making sales rather than on satisfying customers' needs. It frequently results in companies selling products which do not satisfy customer needs.

A **product** is an object, like a television set.

A **service** is different to a product in four respects. First, a service is intangible: it cannot be touched. Second, it is inseparable; which means that production and consumption occur at the same time. Third, it is perishable: it cannot be stored. Fourth, it is variable; this means that the quality of a service depends a great deal on the personnel who deliver it. A mortgage facility or a piano lesson are examples of services.

A **consumer** is the final user of a product or service.

A **customer** is someone who uses, purchases or recommends a product. In this sense, British residents are customers when they make use of hospital facilities, even though hospital treatment is free at the point of use.

The marketing orientation

We have said that the marketing orientation is concerned with the identification and satisfaction of customers' needs. P Kotler has this definition of marketing:

> **Marketing is a human activity directed at satisfying needs and wants through exchange processes.**

Another definition is that offered by P Drucker:

> **Marketing is the whole business seen from the point of view of its final result, that is from the customer's point of view.**

The Chartered Institute of Marketing (CIM) provides this definition:

> **Marketing is the management process which identifies, anticipates and supplies customer requirements efficiently and profitably.**

The Chartered Institute of Marketing's definition is perhaps more useful because it emphasises the relationship between satisfying customers and company profitability. We shall see later in this book, however, that even this definition of marketing is not regarded as satisfactory by all analysts.

A company with a genuine marketing orientation accepts the philosophy that company profitability results from the satisfaction of customers' needs. It seeks to co-ordinate all company activities to achieve the objective of customer satisfaction. Before describing marketing processes in greater detail, it is worth pausing to consider how widespread the marketing orientation really is in Britain. Peter Doyle carried out a study in 1987 into this question, consulting 365 chief executives of leading companies. He concluded that in only 50 per cent of cases could the companies' corporate philosophy be described as marketing orientated. The production and sales orientations are still a feature of business life, despite their acknowledged weaknesses and inadequacies.

 # The marketing department's functions

Marketing-orientated companies above a certain size usually establish a specialist marketing department. In the early days of the marketing era there was a tendency to establish the marketing department alongside the sales department, but it is more usual nowadays to allocate sales as a sub-function within the marketing department.

The functions of the marketing department are to analyse, plan, implement and control marketing activities. Marketing analysis seeks to identify potential customers and to understand their product needs. It also seeks to gain information about the market and any competitors. Marketing analysis may make use of both qualitative and quantitative studies. These are discussed further in Chapter 8.

The data from marketing analysis is used to prepare the company's strategic marketing plan, which will set out the selected target markets, forecast future demand for each target market, and establish the levels of the marketing mix for each one.

The implementation of marketing plans requires staff and financial resources, and activities should be carefully timetabled.

The fourth function of the marketing department is to control the implementation of the strategic marketing plan. This is done by setting measurable performance targets for each part of the plan, and then comparing actual performance against planned performance levels.

 ## The internal environment

In addition to assigning specific responsibilities to the marketing department, it is important to establish a system of formal communication between a company's chief marketing executive and the heads of other departments. It may happen that departments have differing ideas about how to implement company objectives, and these differences need to be discussed and resolved. Some typical inter-departmental conflicts include the following:

The marketing department would like the production department to

◆ reduce its order lead times

◆ have short production runs of great variety

◆ make frequent model changes

◆ impose very high quality control.

The production department, however, would prefer to

◆ maintain long order lead times

◆ have long production runs of limited variety

◆ make minimal model changes

◆ impose average quality control.

In the same way, the marketing department would like the purchasing department to

◆ purchase non-standard parts

◆ purchase according to the quality of materials

◆ maintain large lot sizes for flexible response.

The purchasing department, however, would prefer to

◆ purchase standard parts

◆ purchase according to the price of materials

◆ maintain economic lot sizes.

The marketing department would like

◆ flexible spending programmes

◆ budget adjustments to meet changing needs and circumstances

◆ pricing policies which further market development.

The finance department, however, would like

◆ controlled spending programmes

◆ fixed budgets

◆ pricing policies related to costs.

An aspect of the internal environment that is of crucial importance to a company's potential for success is the development of a positive organisational culture. This means that people in the company share a common perspective about the company, its objectives, and the ways those objectives should be reached. Induction programmes for new employees, and training and seminars for existing personnel, are some of the methods used to engender a positive company culture.

Marketing audits can be used to identify strengths and weaknesses in the internal environment. A marketing audit is an analysis of a company's marketing position and performance. Although marketing audits are also used to examine wider issues, they can be an effective tool for looking at the following aspects of the internal environment:

1 Strengths and weaknesses of the company's marketing activities, known as a SWOT analysis: An audit of this kind might obtain data on the marketing department's response time to problems, on the company's image vis-à-vis customers, suppliers or retail outlets, and measures of customer loyalty. SWOT analysis is discussed further in Chapters 3 and 14.

2 Marketing performance evaluation: An audit of this kind might obtain data on the marketing department's actual performance compared to planned performance in areas such as sales levels.

 ## The marketing mix

A marketing plan depends for its success on what are called the four P's of the marketing mix. These four variables are *Product*, *Price*, *Promotion* and *Place*. All of these are under the control of the company, in the sense that the company is responsible for making decisions about them; although frequently pressures from outside the company influence the decisions that are made. The constituents of the marketing mix are shown in Fig. 1.1. Each of the four elements interacts with the other three, and decisions therefore have to be co-ordinated carefully to arrive at a final marketing mix.

 ## Marketing structures

We saw earlier that the effective implementation of marketing plans depends on good communication between company departments, and on measures which reduce the possibility of inter-departmental conflict. The structure of a marketing department should take these factors into account, as well as the company's general structure, the range and diversity of its products, and the area which it serves. The following are some of the commonest marketing department structures.

Product Features Quality Brand Packaging Durability After-sales service	**Price** Price level Credit terms Discounts Allowances Trade-ins
Promotion Advertising Personal selling Merchandising Publicity	**Place** Distribution channels Coverage intensity Location Stockholding Freight and insurance

Fig. 1.1 Constituents of the marketing mix

 ## Functional structures

The simplest structure is known as the *functional structure*, in which, as Fig. 1.2 illustrates, each marketing function has a separate manager who is accountable to the head of the department.

The advantages of the functional structure are that it is simple and easy to administer, with a clear definition of duties and responsibilities. Its disadvantages are that it is not suited to companies which have a large range of products or serve a large number of markets. This is because of the tendency for managers to concentrate their attention on some products and markets at the expense of others.

 ## Product-based structures

Product-based structures are those in which individual managers are given responsibility for specific products or 'brands'. Figure 1.3 illustrates a typical product-based structure.

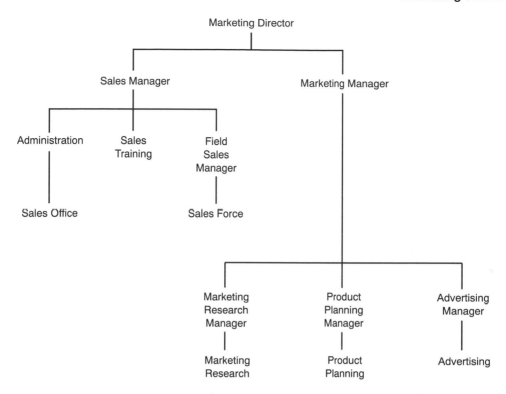

Fig. 1.2 Functional structure of marketing department

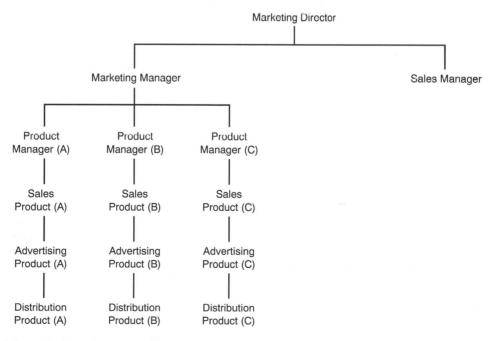

Fig. 1.3 Product-based structure of marketing department

The advantages of product-based structures are that they ensure that marketing activities are focused on diverse product types, and that managers have an opportunity to gain in-depth product experience. Its disadvantages are that 'brand' managers may be negatively competitive with each other, and the structure can lead to an over-emphasis on product knowledge rather than market focus.

 ## Market-based structures

Market-based structures are those in which marketing managers take responsibility for different markets rather than for different products. In some market structures, responsibilities are allocated on a geographical basis; in others allocation is made according to customer type. A market structure is illustrated in Fig. 1.4.

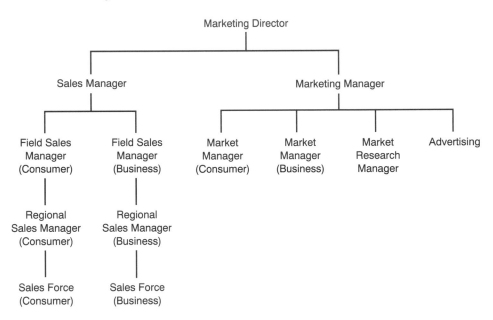

Fig. 1.4 Market structure of marketing department

A particular market structure worthy of note is known as *key account management*. This occurs where a company has some large customers of such importance that special marketing programmes are designed for them. A food company selling its products to one or more supermarkets may select this option for dealing with its largest customers.

The advantages of market structures are that they allow a company to focus its marketing activities on customer groups, and to respond speedily to customer requirements. The disadvantages are that market structures call for considerable investment in personnel, and that it is sometimes difficult to co-ordinate marketing efforts.

 ## Matrix structures

Most large companies choose to organise their marketing activities by 'marrying' simple structures into a *matrix* form. In a simple matrix the department might be organised partly by products and partly by markets. This results in product managers having responsibility for the marketing of a product range, and marketing managers having responsibility for customer groups or markets. A matrix structure of this sort is illustrated in Fig. 1.5.

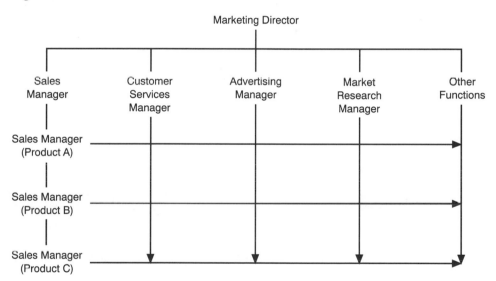

Fig. 1.5 Matrix structure of marketing department

The advantages of matrix structures are that they allow for greater co-ordination between different functions, and for shared decision-making. Disadvantages include the cost of establishing matrix structures and the possibility of inter-departmental conflict and hostility.

 ## Divisional structures

Divisionalisation occurs when a company establishes separate corporate entities, usually under some centralised planning or advisory body. Some companies establish divisions according to product types or some other variable.

Challenges to the marketing concept

As we shall see in later chapters, the traditional marketing concept has been challenged in recent years, and these criticisms have led to an enrichment of marketing theory.

The first of these challenges concerns the marketing assumption that consumers know what they want, and that the task of companies is to identify needs and then satisfy them. It has been suggested that companies which take this view are more likely to follow conventional product development programmes than companies which seek to 'create' needs by developing new products.

Second, it has become clear that not all consumer needs should be met by companies, particularly where to do so would damage the interests of consumers themselves, perhaps by causing environmental harm. We shall look at the relationship between marketing and environmental concerns in Chapters 4 and 6.

Self-assessment test questions

These questions have been designed to test your recall of the main points in this chapter. The answers can be found on page 218.

Complete the following sentences:

1 The most important characteristics of an exchange relationship are . . .

2 The three trade developments which occur as societies become more complex are . . .

3 The problem facing American business between the 1850s and the 1920s was . . .

4 After the 1920s the problem facing American business was . . .

5 The production orientation can be defined as . . .

6 The sales orientation can be defined as . . .

7 The marketing orientation can be defined as . . .

8 The functions of a marketing department are . . .

9 In a functional structure, each marketing function has . . .

10 Market-based structures are those in which managers take responsibility for . . .

State whether each of the following statements is TRUE or FALSE:

11 An exchange relationship consists of two or more parties.

12 The use of money simplifies the exchange process.

13 The Industrial Revolution in Britain began in the 1850s.

14 The word 'market' has no clear meaning.

15 There are four elements to the marketing mix.

Write short notes to answer the following:

16 What is an exchange relationship?

17 What is the 'division of labour'?

18 How did the production orientation come about?

19 How did the sales orientation come about?

20 What are the chief characteristics of the marketing orientation?

 Research activity

You remember from the text that Professor Peter Doyle carried out some research to determine certain leading companies' commitment to the marketing approach.

Select one or two businesses in your area and assess their approach to the market. Present your findings to the group.

Relationships

2

After reading this chapter you should be able to:

◆ **List the four principal ways in which markets can be defined**

◆ **Identify the five competitive forces in M E Porter's competition model**

◆ **Describe the principal ways in which products are distributed**

◆ **Explain the main influences on consumer behaviour.**

In Chapter 1 we looked at the origins of marketing, and at some of the ways in which a marketing department can be organised. We also looked at the internal environment within which marketing activities take place, and at some of the problems that can arise in that environment. In this chapter we are moving outside the company to consider the *micro-environment* within which the company operates. The relationship between the internal environment and the micro-environment is illustrated in Fig. 2.1.

The micro-, or market environment, unlike the internal environment discussed in Chapter 1, is more difficult to manage because it contains some entities which are outside the company's immediate control. It is important for a company to understand the dynamics of this environment, however, so that it can develop informed strategies for meeting its objectives.

Market structures

One of the most essential tasks a company must do before it can formulate a marketing strategy is to define the market or markets it wishes to serve. In Chapter 1 we saw that marketers define a 'market' as the buyers of a product or service. The car market, then, is made up of all car buyers, and the clothes market is made up of all those who buy clothes. This definition of a market is too general to be of much practical use to an individual company

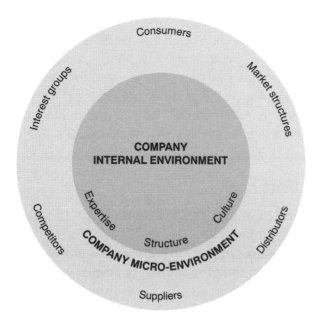

Fig. 2.1 Relationship between internal environment and micro-environment

because very few companies serve an entire market. Rolls-Royce and Landrover cars, for example, are both involved in the car market, as Marks & Spencer and Versace are both involved in the clothes market. This does not mean that Rolls-Royce is in direct competition with Landrover, or Marks & Spencer with Versace. Each of these companies serves a distinct 'part' of the total market. Let us look at the various ways in which the 'parts' of a total market can be defined.

Product-based definitions

Many markets are defined by reference to products, as the following examples show:

◆ the car market

◆ the clothes market

◆ the boat market

◆ the camera market.

Although product-based definitions of markets are widely used, they ignore the fact that customers are seeking needs-satisfiers rather than simply products when they make a purchase. This point was made by T Levitt in a famous article, 'Marketing Myopia', published in 1960. Levitt argued that the reason the American railway companies lost their passenger and freight businesses to trucking companies and airlines was that the railway companies saw themselves as being in the railway business rather than in the transportation business. In other words, they defined their market in product terms rather than in terms of customers' needs.

 ## Need-based definitions

According to Levitt, market definitions should be made in terms of 'that which the customer buys' rather than in terms of 'what the organisation or industry makes'. As an example of this failure to define markets in terms of customer needs, Levitt argued that film industry planners saw their market in terms of films rather than in terms of entertainment. For this reason, they failed to predict the threat from television which fulfilled the same need they were serving.

Although the need-based approach has reminded companies that they should look at markets from a customer-orientated perspective, it is not always easy to arrive at a satisfactory need-based definition of a market. We will come back to this point later in this chapter when we consider A H Maslow's needs hierarchy.

 ## Consumer markets and organisational markets

Another approach to defining markets is to divide them into *consumer markets* and *organisational markets*. Consumer markets are made up of people who purchase products for personal or home use. Consumers generally buy from retail outlets, and their purchases are of relatively low value. Organisational markets are made up of businesses, government organisations and institutions. Purchasing is not normally carried out in retail outlets, and purchases are of relatively high value.

 ## Purchases

Markets can also be defined by the types of purchase made. One method of defining markets by reference to purchase-types classifies purchases according to their physical tangibility:

◆ *Durables* are products designed to last for at least one year, such as washing-machines.

◆ *Non-durables* are products with a life of less than one year, such as ball-point pens.

◆ *Services* are intangible items such as legal advice or beauty treatment.

A second method of defining markets by reference to purchase-types classifies purchases according to the way in which the purchase is made:

◆ *Convenience goods* are products of low value which tend to be bought habitually or on impulse. Examples include basic foods and toiletries.

◆ *Shopping goods* are products of higher value which are purchased after a more systematic search for good value. Examples include foreign holidays and exotic foods.

◆ *Speciality goods* are products about which the customer has a deeper knowledge, and the purchase decision is not conditioned mainly by price. Examples include sporting equipment and collectables.

As well as defining its market, a company needs to make an estimate of the current size of the market, its potential size, and how quickly the market is growing. We will look at these aspects of the market more fully in Chapters 12 and 13.

 ## Competitors

The business world today is very competitive, and marketing managers need to familiarise themselves with their company's competitors before committing resources to their own marketing strategies. We will look at competitor analysis in some detail in Chapter 7.

Economists have traditionally approached the subject of competition by examining how markets are structured in terms of the number of sellers. This kind of analysis leads to the following types of competitive industry structure:

Monopoly

A monopoly exists when there is only one seller. Customer choice is limited solely to whether or not to make a purchase. Before privatisation the railway system in Britain was a monopoly.

Oligopoly

An oligopoly exists where there are a few sellers. Customer choice is a little wider than in a monopoly, but it is still restricted. In the 1970s Sir Freddie Laker's airline 'Skytrain' offered cheaper trans-Atlantic flights than the major carriers. His efforts to break their oligopoly failed, because his competitors lowered their prices as well, knowing that they could afford to lose money for longer than the smaller airline.

Perfect competition

Perfect competition exists where there are many sellers competing for customers on equal terms.

Their approach to competition, in terms of number of sellers, is useful from a theoretical point of view, but does not provide sufficient data to be of great value in the development of marketing strategies. We shall return to a discussion of economic theory in Chapters 11 and 12.

An alternative approach is provided by M E Porter. M E Porter argues that competition within an industry depends on the economic structure of that industry, more than it does on the behaviour of competing companies. According to this analysis, competition is the result of five competitive forces. These forces determine an industry's long-term profit potential. The five competitive forces identified by Porter are:

1 *The threat of new entrants to the industry* New entrants increase the competitiveness of an industry. The number of new entrants to an industry is partly determined by the existence of entry barriers, and partly by the response of existing competitors to new entrants. Entry barriers include the following:

    (a) *Economies of scale* Obviously it is more difficult for a company to enter an industry which is dominated by a few large competitors whose operating costs benefit from economies of scale.

    (b) *Product differentiation and brand identity* Again, it is difficult for a new company to enter an industry in which there is already a good range of products and some established leading brands.

    (c) *Capital requirements* Entry to an industry is made more difficult when start-up costs, in the form of capital requirements, are very high.

    (d) *Access to distribution* It is difficult to enter some industries because product distribution is dominated by companies serving competitors, and the cost of establishing a distribution system is prohibitive.

2 *Suppliers* The bargaining strength of suppliers is greater when:

   (a) There are only a few suppliers, and they are more concentrated than the industry which they serve.

   (b) Suppliers do not have to compete with other products to sell to the industry.

   (c) The suppliers do not see the industry as one of their important customer groups.

3 *Buyers* The bargaining strength of buyers is greater when:

   (a) Buyers are concentrated, or they make volume purchases.

   (b) Buyers prefer standard products.

   (c) The products which buyers purchase are unimportant to the final quality of the buyers' own products.

   (d) Buyers have the chance to make the industry's product themselves.

4 *Substitute products* These exist when a customer can 'switch' between two similar products if the price of one of them rises. The existence of substitute products establishes a price maximum, and can mean that companies are able to enter a market by offering a substitute product at a lower price.

5 *Industry competitors* The intensity of competitor rivalry is affected by the following factors:

   (a) *The concentration of the industry* If there are many competitors of equal size, then competition will be more intense.

   (b) *Industrial growth* If the rate of growth is slow, then competition will be more intense, as companies fight for market share.

   (c) *Exit barriers* If it is difficult for companies to leave the market, then competition will be more intense.

 ## Suppliers and distributors

An essential part of a company's marketing strategy concerns making products available to customers. Product distribution is the fourth of the marketing mix variables encountered in Chapter 1: *place*. Other terms used for place include distribution, delivery systems and marketing channels. The most important distributive functions are:

◆ transport

◆ storage and stockholding

◆ promotion

◆ display

◆ pricing

◆ selling

◆ credit facilities

◆ after-sales service.

Figure 2.2 shows the various ways in which a product can be distributed from a company to its customers.

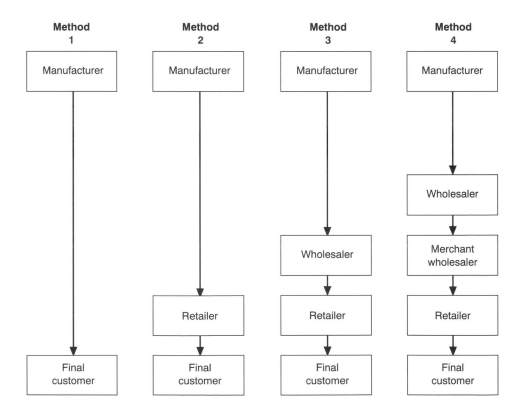

Fig. 2.2 Product distribution methods

In method 1, the manufacturer takes control of the distribution process. No intermediaries are involved in the process, which is known as a *direct channel*. The high street banks, along with most industrial goods manufacturers, prefer to use the direct channel approach in the distribution of their products to customers.

The majority of manufacturers use intermediaries because they want to reduce costs and increase sales. Intermediaries reduce manufacturers' costs in the following ways:

◆ Contacts between manufacturers and customers are reduced, thus reducing the manufacturers' transport costs (see Figs. 2.3 and 2.4).

◆ Manufacturers do not have the expense of maintaining product stocks.

◆ Manufacturers do not have the expense of sales administration.

◆ Manufacturers do not have to maintain a huge sales force.

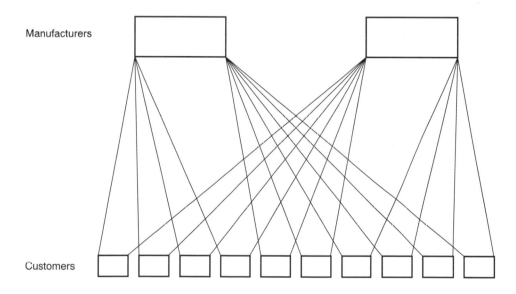

Fig. 2.3 Direct channel of distribution with maximum transport costs for manufacturer

Intermediaries increase manufacturers' sales in the following ways:

◆ They are geographically placed so that the products are accessible to customers.

◆ They have a greater knowledge of customer requirements in their geographical area than manufacturers do.

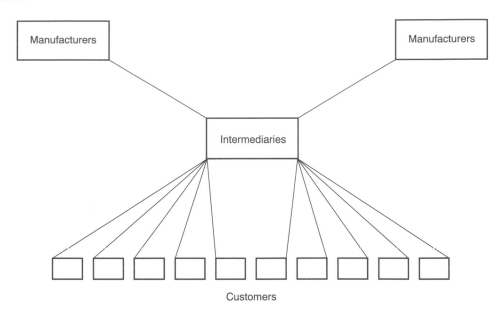

Fig. 2.4 Using intermediaries reduces manufacturers' contact with customers and hence transport costs

◆ They are specialised in making products available to customers, which manufacturers are often not.

In method 2 there is one intermediary between the manufacturer and the customers, which is the retailer. In method 3 there are two intermediaries between the manufacturer and the customers: a wholesaler and a retailer. In method 4 there are three intermediaries between the manufacturer and the customers: a wholesaler, a retailer and a merchant wholesaler.

There are different kinds of intermediary. Some intermediaries take legal ownership of the products which they sell on, whereas others act as agents. These different roles are listed below:

◆ *Agents* do not take title to goods, but negotiate contracts of sale for their principals.

◆ *Merchants* take title to goods, either as wholesalers or retailers. Wholesalers generally stock a range of goods from different suppliers, which they sell on to retail outlets. The majority of wholesalers deal in consumer goods, although some also specialise in industrial goods. Retailers sell directly to households. Retailers can be classified by the kind of goods they sell, the type of service they offer, and their size and location. Another way of classifying retailers is whether they are independent or part of a multiple chain.

◆ *Dealers* take title to products and resell them at wholesale or retail.

◆ *Distributors* take title to products and sell them on to dealers for eventual distribution to retailers.

◆ *Franchisees* are independent organisations which trade under the name of a parent organisation under a licensing arrangement.

Channel network strategies

A company's choice of a channel network for the distribution and sale of its goods to customers will be influenced by a number of factors, particularly the degree of market exposure it wishes to obtain. Fundamental network strategies can be classified as follows:

1 *Intensive distribution* This is a strategy which aims to make the product available in the maximum number of outlets. It is particularly used in the distribution of products which are purchased frequently, such as petrol or cigarettes, or 'impulse' buys such as soft drinks. For such purposes the image of the retail outlet is not a major factor in determining the purchase.

2 *Selective distribution* This is a strategy which aims to ensure that the product is sold only through profitable outlets, or through reputable outlets whose image will not damage the manufacturer's reputation. Washing machine and television manufacturers, for example, want their products to be widely available, but nevertheless establish retail outlet criteria.

3 *Exclusive distribution* This is a strategy which aims to restrict the number of retail outlets in a given area in order to enhance the prestige of a product by ensuring that dealers or outlets provide a very high level of customer service. Luxury cars such as Rolls-Royce and Porsche, and other prestigious products, are distributed in this way.

Marketing channel flows

In conventional marketing channels, suppliers and intermediaries are independent organisations which are connected by complex 'flows', as Fig. 2.5 illustrates. Some of these flows move down-channel, while others move up-channel; others still move in both directions.

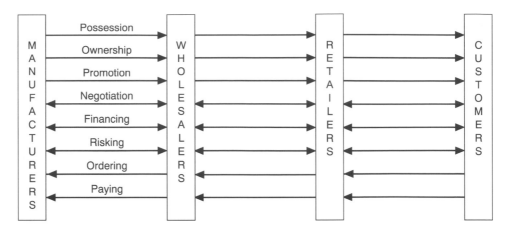

Fig. 2.5 Marketing channel flows between suppliers and intermediaries

 Marketing channel conflict

Although it might seem that all channel members share common goals in the establishment of a co-ordinated and efficient system, channel conflict is not infrequent. Conflict usually arises because channel members are separate legal entities, and each has its own distinct interests. J C Palamountain has identified three types of channel conflict:

1 *Horizontal conflict* occurs when there is competition between intermediaries operating at the same channel level. Two retail outlets which stock the same product would be an example of this kind of conflict.

2 *Intertype conflict* occurs when intermediaries at the same channel level begin to trade in products outside their normal product range. Garages which stock grocery products provide an example of this kind of conflict.

3 *Vertical conflict* occurs when there is competition between intermediaries at different channel levels. A wholesaler who decides to sell products at reduced prices to consumers, instead of leaving this function to retailers, is an example of this kind of conflict.

Typical causes of conflict include the following:

◆ *Failure to agree common goals or agree ways to achieve common goals* Although all channel members will want to co-operate to maximise profitability, there may well be disagreement over how profits should be apportioned between channel members. Again, although channel members are likely to agree that product volume should be increased, disagreement may arise over how much of a product should be stored by wholesalers and how much should be displayed in retail outlets.

◆ *Different views of reality* Each channel member is likely to approach problems in a different way, because each channel member is a specialist in its own field. Failure to understand the perceptions and assumptions of other channel members can lead to conflict. A retailer, for example, may prefer to make frequent, small orders for products because of shelf-size limits; whereas a manufacturer may prefer to provide less frequent, larger deliveries.

◆ *Failure to communicate* Sometimes a manufacturer will withold information about planned new products from other channel members until the last moment. Other channel members then have to formulate their own strategies hurriedly.

 ## Channel member strengths

We saw earlier that Rolls-Royce and Porsche are in a strong enough position to set the conditions in which dealers will operate. In such a relationship, the suppliers' strength is greater than that of the intermediaries. In other cases, however, intermediaries are stronger than suppliers. This is the case with the major supermarket retailers, who can set the conditions in which their suppliers operate. In these examples the relative strengths of suppliers and intermediaries are acknowledged, and working relationships can be negotiated. In some markets, however, where rapid and profound changes are taking place, conflict between channel levels is inevitable as channel members jockey for position. In the book trade, for example, the movement towards the abolition of the Net Book Agreement, and the domination of retailing by W H Smith and other chains such as Dillons, have resulted in ambiguity about the relative bargaining strengths of publishers and retailers.

 ## Vertical marketing systems

We have seen that the conventional marketing systems can lead to channel members competing against each other and so to channel conflict. In a vertical marketing system, manufacturers and intermediaries co-ordinate marketing channels in order to work together to achieve common goals and to eliminate conflict. A vertical marketing system only works when one channel member is given leadership status by the other members.

In a corporate vertical marketing system, one channel member owns one or more of the other channel members. Although this kind of vertical integration is expensive to establish, it brings the following benefits:

◆ economies of scale

◆ co-ordinated marketing efforts

◆ barriers to entry.

Vertical integration can be achieved through contractual arrangements, as well as through ownership of channel participants. Franchises, co-operatives and voluntary groups are all examples of this kind of vertical system.

 # Consumers

In Chapter 1 we saw that marketing is about the identification and satisfaction of customer needs. It is therefore of great importance for a company to understand its customers, whether these are consumers or other organisations. In this chapter we will look at the major influences on consumer buying behaviour. Organisational buying behaviour is discussed in Chapter 13.

 # Consumer buying behaviour

It used to be thought that consumer buying behaviour was a rational process in which the consumer compared different products by reference to product performance and reliability, availability and price, and made a purchase decision according to these. In fact very little consumer buying is carried out in this way, and more sophisticated models of the process have been developed which take account of other factors. Figure 2.6 shows some of the variables involved in the consumer purchase decision.

 # Environmental influences on consumers

Marketing communications, in the form of advertisements, shop displays, and so on, are a characteristic feature of modern societies. It is from these communications that consumers gather some of the information about companies and products which influences their buying behaviour. Marketing stimuli can be analysed by reference to the four P's of the marketing mix: product, price, promotion and place. Companies can manipulate the elements in the marketing mix to influence consumer behaviour.

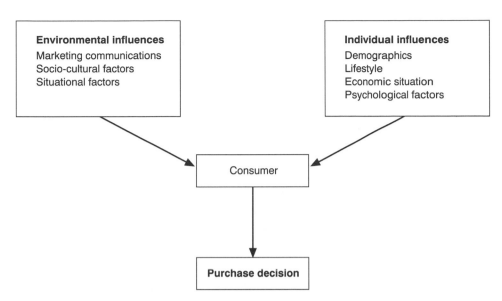

Fig. 2.6 Variables involved in customer purchase decision

Socio-cultural influences express a society's fundamental beliefs, attitudes, values and behavioural norms. Core cultural values and secondary values are discussed in greater detail in Chapter 3. The socio-cultural influences which are particularly relevant to consumer buying behaviour are social class, and primary and secondary reference groups.

Social classes are groups within a society who share economic or social characteristics. Members of the same social class tend to share behavioural patterns, beliefs and values. Social class groupings can be made according to occupation, educational attainment or income. Social class is a major determinant of the kinds of products people buy, and also of where purchases are made.

Primary reference groups are those people with whom a consumer most often associates, and include family, friends and work colleagues. Within the family, individual members may assume any of the following purchase roles:

◆ information gatherer

◆ influencer

◆ decision maker

◆ purchaser

◆ consumer.

In the case of a Christmas toy, for example, a child's brother or sister might be the information gatherer, the mother the decision maker, the father the purchaser, and the child the consumer.

Secondary reference groups are those people with whom a consumer has less contact, and may include members of social clubs, fellow church members, or other associates. Aspirational groups are those to which a consumer would like to belong, and dissociative groups are those to which a consumer would not wish to belong.

Both primary and secondary reference groups influence individual consumer behaviour by shaping self-image and attitudes, by exposing individuals to new behaviour, and by exerting pressure to conform to behavioural norms.

Situational factors also influence consumer behaviour. Airport shopping centres are designed to appeal to airline passengers and offer a range of products to meet the needs of consumers in this situation: cafés and restaurants, gifts and everyday items. The duty-free sections of airports, however, tend to offer a more expensive range of products to air travellers: perfumes, alcohol, cameras and electronic equipment.

Individual influences

Consumer purchase behaviour is influenced by four important psychological factors: motivation, perception, learning processes and attitudes.

Motivation

Marketers are interested in discovering what motivates consumers when they purchase products, and there are two ways in which researchers have sought to gain insights into this aspect of behaviour.

1 Motivational research, which is a technique based on the Freudian approach to psychology, uses in-depth interviews in an attempt to uncover the unconscious motives behind consumer behaviour.

2 A second approach follows the model of motivation proposed by A H Maslow. Figure 2.7 shows Maslow's hierarchy of needs. According to this model, human needs are hierarchical, and individuals move from the satisfaction of lower-level needs to the satisfaction of higher-level needs.

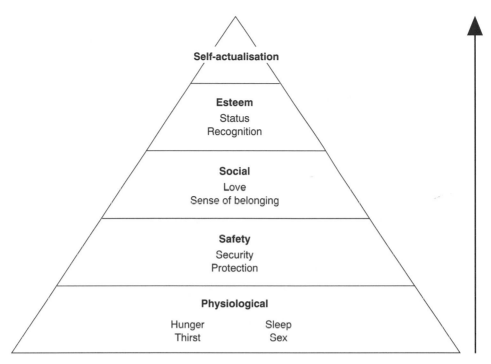

Fig. 2.7 Maslow's hierarchy of needs

Perception

Perception is the way in which people interpret the world around them. Marketers need to understand how it happens that similarly-motivated people may act in different ways. Three perceptual phenomena are of particular interest:

1 *Selective perception* occurs when an individual ignores some of the information in the world around him because of information overload. Selective perception also describes the two phenomena by which individuals are likely to notice expected stimuli and to be struck by unusual stimuli. Advertisers use their knowledge of selective perception when they include surprising visual images or text in advertisements.

2 *Selective distortion* occurs when an individual interprets data in ways that have personal significance. A consumer who has been told by a friend, for example, that a product is unreliable, is unlikely to believe a salesperson's glowing report on its record of reliability.

3 *Selective retention* occurs when individuals remember only that information which supports their own attitudes and beliefs.

Learning processes

Learning can be defined as the changes which occur in an individual's behaviour as a result of experience. If a consumer buys a product and is satisfied with the purchase, the purchase is said to be *positively reinforced*. If the consumer repeats the purchase in the future, the reinforcement is said to be *generalised*. The implication of learning theory for marketers is that products should be designed to satisfy strong drives, and that purchase decisions should be positively reinforced.

Attitudes

Attitudes are favourable or unfavourable views of a company or product. It is very difficult to change consumer attitudes once these have been formed.

Demographic variables classify people according to age, sex, income, occupation, education and life-cycle stage. Demographic variables influence not only the kind of products consumers buy, but where they make purchases and the criteria by which they appraise the purchasing process.

Lifestyle variables include an individual's activities, interests and opinions, all of which influence consumer behaviour.

Economic situation refers to how much money an individual has to spend, and also to such matters as the individual's borrowing capacity and attitude to spending.

 ## Interest groups

Interest groups, which are sometimes also referred to as *publics* or *stakeholders*, are the final sector within a company's micro-environment. P Kotler has defined publics in this way:

> **A public is any group that has an actual or potential interest in, or impact on, a company's ability to achieve its objectives.**

A company's typical publics include the following:

◆ *Shareholders* It is essential to shareholder confidence that a company communicates effectively with investors and explains problems and strategies to them.

◆ *Financial institutions* Lenders will require full details of company objectives before committing themselves to projects requiring capital loans.

◆ *The local community* Most companies wish to enjoy good relations with the community of which they form a part. Increasingly, such relationships are becoming dependent as much on environmental matters as the fostering of good employment practices.

◆ *The general public* A company's public image is inseparable from the image the public holds of its products. There has been a tendency in recent years, particularly in America, for the general public to express concerns about company activities by boycotting products.

◆ *The news media* The development of good press relations is one of the functions of the marketing department.

◆ *Government departments and regulatory bodies* Good relations here depend on effective communication with supervisory bodies.

We will return to the subject of stakeholders in Chapter 4.

Self-assessment test questions

These questions have been designed to test your recall of the main points in this chapter. The answers can be found on p. 218.

Complete the following sentences:

1 The market environment is more difficult to manage than the internal environment because . . .

2 According to T Levitt, market definitions should be made in terms of . . .

3 One method of defining markets is to classify purchases as durables, non-durables and . . .

4 Perfect competition exists where there are . . .

5 A direct channel is one in which . . .

6 The three fundamental channel network strategies are . . .

7 Conflict between channel members usually arises because . . .

8 A vertical marketing system works only when . . .

9 Primary reference groups are . . .

10 The four psychological factors which influence consumer behaviour are . . .

State whether each of the following statements is TRUE or FALSE:

11 Product definitions of markets ignore the fact that customers are seeking needs-satisfiers rather than products.

12 Convenience goods are frozen food products sold in supermarkets.

13 A monopoly is a term used for a state-run industry.

14 M E Porter has defined six competitive forces.

15 Interest groups lobby politicians for product and company changes.

Write short notes on the following:

16 (a) product-based definitions of markets

    (b) purchase definitions of markets

17 (a) the bargaining strength of suppliers

    (b) the bargaining strength of buyers

18 the functions of intermediaries

19 vertical marketing systems

20 interest groups.

Discussion activity

Consider the following products:

◆ cellular telephone

◆ designer jeans

◆ engagement ring

◆ smoke detector

◆ bread.

Use A H Maslow's hierarchy of needs to determine which needs these products satisfy. Compare your results with those of other students in the group. How easy is it to define markets in terms of customer needs?

Market forces

After reading this chapter you should be able to:

◆ **Explain the importance of the PEST factors**

◆ **Describe what is meant by SWOT analysis**

◆ **Outline the principal purposes and techniques of environmental scanning.**

In Chapter 1 we looked at the internal environment in which a company operates, and in Chapter 2 we went on to look at its micro-environment. In this chapter we will consider macro-environmental forces.

It is usual to examine a company's macro-environmental factors under the four headings of Politics, Economics, Society and Technology (PEST). Figure 3.1 illustrates how these four areas can be further sub-divided to include the consideration of other factors. The first thing to notice about macro-environmental factors is that they are beyond the control of a single company.

The political and legal environment

The basic conditions in which businesses operate are established by a country's political and legal system. This system makes certain activities possible and constrains or forbids others.

Political systems differ enormously, both according to their fundamental philosophy or ideology, and their view of the purpose of business activity. Government economic policies have an enormous effect on business confidence.

The former Soviet Union was markedly less democratic in structure than the liberal democracies of the USA and Europe. Furthermore, it saw business activity as something to be centrally planned and organised. The concept of wealth was defined in terms of 'common ownership' rather than personal self-enrichment. Western companies dealing with purchasing officers from

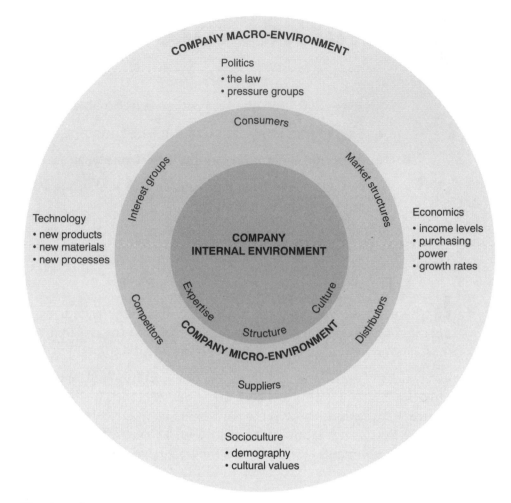

Fig. 3.1 Company's macro-environmental factors

the USSR often found that decision-making was a lengthy process, and that decisions were frequently made on non-commercial grounds. Contract negotiations were made more difficult still by the problems associated with the value of the rouble.

These difficulties should be contrasted with the political environment of Britain during the years of the Thatcher government. The government placed great emphasis on the importance of business, and removed government controls, as well as embarking on a prolonged programme of privatisation. Business confidence grew, partly as a result of the government's positive attitude.

Political instability is also a factor which has a serious effect on business activity. Some countries are prone to sudden changes of government, outbreaks of civil war, or political uncertainty. Companies are generally reluctant to export to regions such as these, where there is always the possibility that a political change will intervene disastrously in the performance of a contract.

In recent years investment in Hong Kong has fluctuated because of uncertainties over the intentions of the Chinese government when it assumes control of the former British colony in 1997. Despite reassurances to investors from both the British and Chinese negotiators, considerable doubts still remain, and until these are finally removed, business activity in Hong Kong is unlikely to increase dramatically.

Although companies would obviously prefer to centre their activities in democratic countries whose governments have a favourable view towards business activity, marketing-orientated companies will still seek opportunities wherever they occur. The former Soviet Union, for example, was a source of lucrative joint-ventures between western companies and the government. In the same way, many foreign companies were keen to maintain their links with South Africa, despite their disapproval of the apartheid system.

Legislation is the principal means by which governments control business operating conditions, although regulatory bodies also have a role in the supervision of business activities.

Products which are permissible in some countries are forbidden in others: the magazine 'Playboy', for example, is not permitted in certain Arab countries because it is considered an obscene publication. Similarly, handguns can be purchased in gunsmiths relatively easily in certain American states, whereas in Britain there is a much tighter licensing system. Sometimes there are legal rules governing how products must be sold: antibiotics are available from Italian chemists without a doctor's prescription, whereas in Britain they have to be prescribed. Laws governing shop opening hours differ from one country to another, as do laws governing the sale of alcoholic drinks.

Legislation is also used to control competition and monopolies, and to protect the interests of consumers. In Britain these functions are controlled by the *Office of Fair Trading* and the *Monopolies and Mergers Commission*. Articles 85 and 86 of the Treaty of Rome also cover these matters. There are a number of Acts of Parliament covering consumer protection, including:

◆ The Trades Description Act, 1973

◆ The Consumer Credit Act, 1974

◆ The Unfair Contract Terms Act, 1977.

In addition there is further legislation covering such areas as sales promotions, product guarantees, weights and measures, and food safety.

British businesses not only monitor political events at home, they must also monitor events taking place within the European Union (EU). The European Commission suggests policy changes to the European Parliament and to the Economic and Social Committee. Suggestions for change are then passed on to the Council of Ministers, which issues a directive. After inspection by the Court of Justice, suggestions for change are then issued in the form of directives, regulations or decisions. These all have legal force in the member states of the Union.

Some of the most important policies of the European Union are listed here:

1 *Competition policy* This policy is designed to remove and prevent tariff and non-tariff barriers to trade between member states, to monitor trade monopolies, and to prevent member states' domestic policies from distorting free competition.

2 *Agricultural policy* This policy is designed to ensure an adequate supply of food for member states, to provide a fair standard of living for farmers, and to increase agricultural productivity.

3 *Regional policy* This policy is designed to encourage the poorer regions within the Union. The policy has been contentious because its use of subsidies and grants is seen by some to work against the principle of the competition policy.

4 *Social policy* This policy is designed to achieve mobility of labour between member states, to standardise safety legislation, and to harmonise employment legislation.

5 C*onsumer policy* This policy is designed to protect consumer interests, and to provide consumer information and education.

As well as being obliged to act according to specific pieces of legislation, many professions and industries have adopted voluntary codes of practice in an effort to guarantee standards of conduct. The British Medical Association, the Law Society, and the Chartered Institute of Marketing, all oblige their members to abide by a code of practice.

Pressure groups and voluntary associations also exert an influence on companies to change their way of doing things. Some pressure groups, such as the anti-smoking body, ASH, succeed in persuading the government to introduce new legislation. The ecological pressure group Greenpeace has had considerable success in focusing public attention on issues such as whaling, the disposal of dangerous waste and the testing of nuclear weapons. Industries have frequently responded to campaigns organised by pressure groups. The use of aerosol propellants which do not harm the ozone layer came about as the result of lobbying by pressure groups.

 ## The economic environment

As mentioned previously, the economic environment of an individual country is closely related to its political and legal environment. In addition to studying the conditions of the domestic economy, a company needs to be aware of economic trends within regional trade blocs, such as the European Union, and global economic trends. Most large companies incorporate economic data into their Marketing Information System.

The following economic factors are of particular importance to companies:

1 *National income levels* Gross Domestic Product (GDP) is a measure of the value of goods produced within a country. Gross National Product (GNP) is a measure of the value of goods produced within a country and the value of its overseas earnings. GNP therefore provides a more reliable picture of a country's income. GNP by itself, however, is not sufficient to indicate the extent of a country's business opportunities, as it gives no indication of the relationship between wealth and a country's population level. *'Per capita' income* can be obtained by dividing GNP by the number of people in the population.

2 *Purchasing power* Although the calculation of per capita income gives a rough indication of a country's standard of living, it says nothing about how much money the population has to spend on goods after paying government taxes. One measure of purchasing power is obtained by subtracting from per capita income an amount for government taxation, to arrive at what is called *disposable income*. A more useful measure of purchasing power is obtained by making a further subtraction of the cost of necessary expenditure on housing, food and clothing: the figure obtained being called *discretionary income*.

3 *Rate of economic growth* It is important to know whether a country's economy is growing, remaining at about the same level, or declining.

4 *Income distribution* Disposable income and discretionary income are concerned with averages, and give no information about how incomes are distributed between different groups in society. Some countries with low averages for per capita income and discretionary income

nevertheless have a small élite group which is wealthy and therefore has a demand for luxury products. This is particularly true of some third world countries, where there is an enormous gap between rich and poor. Even within European countries, the national income can be distributed in different ways between groups.

5 *Consumption patterns* As well as knowing how wealth is distributed between social groups in a country, it is also important to know how people choose to spend their money. Consumption patterns vary greatly between different countries, according to local culture.

6 *Rate of inflation* A high inflation rate destroys purchasing power and makes it increasingly difficult for companies to set prices or estimate demand.

 ## The sociocultural environment

The marketing environment is affected by a number of sociocultural factors, which a company needs to understand if it is to provide products which satisfy customers' needs and expectations. The most important of these factors are discussed here.

Demographics

Demographics is the study of population. The marketing environment is affected by demographic factors, the most important of which are:

1 *Population levels and age distribution* It is important to know not only whether the population of a country is increasing or decreasing in absolute terms, but how different groups are distributed within the population. In Britain, for example, advances in medicine have helped to increase life-expectancy, while at the same time there has been a slight decrease in the birthrate. This means that Britain has an 'ageing' population: demand for products such as pension plans, medical services for the elderly, and other age-related products, are therefore likely to increase in the future.

2 *Family size and composition* In many advanced economies, couples are marrying later in life than previously, and producing fewer children. In the northern region of Italy, for example, there is a negative birthrate. Changes in work patterns in advanced countries have been a major cause of changes in family size. Many couples, in which both partners have careers, now choose either to delay or to limit the number of children they have, or

decide not to have children at all. There have also been changes in family composition which are of importance to marketers. In Britain, for example, there has been an increase in the number of single-parent families.

3 *Demographic groups* Demographic studies can also provide companies with useful data about population densities for different parts of a country, and about the distribution of wealth between different age groups, regions, social classes and occupational groups. Such studies in Britain, for example, have shown that the size of the traditional working-class declined between 1975–1995.

Core cultural values

Core cultural values express a society's fundamental beliefs, attitudes, values, lifestyle choices and behavioural norms. It is important for a company to understand core cultural values, because these condition not only the kind of products which people want to buy, but also when they buy them, and the use to which they put them.

Core cultural values vary between countries, between regions, and also between social groupings within the same society. Companies engaged in international marketing need to be certain that their advertising campaigns do not offend the cultural sensibilities of audiences in other countries.

Core cultural values change relatively slowly over time, and it is important for companies to be aware of the development of new trends. In Britain, core values which have changed in recent years include those regarding the employment of women and attitudes towards the use of credit.

Secondary cultural values

Secondary cultural values exist below the level of core cultural values, and may be common to all sections of a society, or exhibited by some sections only. Examples of secondary cultural value changes in Britain include the widespread interest in healthier eating, and the change in attitudes towards 'drink-driving'. Less widespread secondary cultural values are associated with sub-cultures, in which particular beliefs, attitudes or lifestyle choices are a feature. Secondary cultural values tend to be less deeply rooted than core values, and to change more rapidly over time.

Aesthetic values

Aesthetic values vary from country to country and companies need to be aware of the aesthetic preferences of their customers. Many British clothes manufacturers who export their products to Europe adapt their designs and colours to appeal to European customers.

The technological environment

We live in a period of very rapid technological change, and companies which remain out of touch with changes in technology will not be able to retain customers.

Technology not only makes new products, it makes new products available to an increasing number of people. New products from the last twenty years include the home computer, the video-cassette player, satellite television, the fax machine and mobile phones.

As well as making new products available, technology also makes old products obsolete, or forces companies to redirect their marketing strategies. Thirty years ago, for example, the technology used in wrist-watches was the spring mechanism. Nowadays, most people prefer battery-operated watches because of their greater accuracy and reliability. Some watch manufacturers, however, have specialised in producing up-market, traditional watches which use the old technology. The same thing has happened in the pen market, where most people prefer a ballpoint pen to the old-fashioned ink fountain-pen. Companies like Parker and Mont Blanc still produce fountain-pens, but these are now marketed as luxury products.

Technology also makes new materials available, such as teflon, carbon fibre optics, and graphite. New materials can be applied to existing products to revolutionise their performance: as in the case of teflon to cooking utensils, carbon fibre optics to telephone cables, and graphite to sports equipment.

Environmental scanning: the internal environment

Our study of the company environment has so far described those factors which are important in the internal environment (Chapter 1), the micro-environment (Chapter 2), and the macro-environment. We now need to consider how a company can utilise data taken from any of these environments in the preparation of its marketing plans.

Before a strategic marketing plan can be formulated, a company needs to assess its own internal resources. This kind of assessment is usually done by carrying out a *SWOT analysis*. SWOT stands for *Strengths*, *Weaknesses*, *Opportunities* and *Threats*. The fundamental purpose of a SWOT analysis is to appraise the relationships between a company's internal strengths and weaknesses, and its external opportunities and threats.

There are different ways to approach the assessment of company strengths and weaknesses. Some companies prepare a checklist of attributes to be assessed under different functional headings, e.g. marketing, production, finance, personnel and research and development. This approach is very costly because it results in a great number of attributes being assessed. It can also be a wasteful approach because some of the attributes assessed will not be strategically significant.

A more effective way of approaching a SWOT analysis is by reference to 'key factors to success'. A company using this approach decides which attributes are most important to its success and assesses these. Although key factors will vary from company to company, typical key factors include financial resources and company skills. It is important that the attributes chosen for assessment are ones which contribute to competitive success. We will look at ways of comparing company strengths with competitors' strengths in Chapter 7. It is also important that the attributes chosen for assessment should relate to customer needs. A company strength that is not perceived as such by customers, or is not valued by them, is not a company strength at all.

An area in which a company excels is known as a *distinctive competence*. Weaknesses are aspects of the company which tend to inhibit the achievement of company objectives. Like strengths, weaknesses should be assessed by reference to competitors, and by reference to customer perceptions, in order to arrive at factors relevant to business success.

Some companies prefer to involve outside consultants in the evaluation of strengths and weaknesses, because there is always the danger that in-house appraisals will be subjective. Sometimes, too, customers can be asked to contribute to an assessment of company strengths and weaknesses by completing questionnaires. Figure 3.2 shows how a SWOT matrix can be constructed.

Once strengths and weaknesses have been identified and assessed, the company can begin to perceive its marketing opportunities and threats. A SWOT analysis allows a company to devise strategies for 'matching' company strengths with opportunities and 'converting' company weaknesses into strengths. External threats can be converted into opportunities by developing relevant, new strengths.

FACTORS WITHIN THE COMPANY

Strengths	**Weaknesses**
Opportunities	**Threats**

FACTORS OUTSIDE THE COMPANY

Fig. 3.2 SWOT matrix

Environmental scanning: the external environment

A scan of the external environment should:

◆ monitor general trends, issues and events in a company's micro-environment (where appropriate, such monitoring activities should also be focused on macro-environmental trends)

◆ identify trends which may have a possible impact on the company

◆ evaluate the significance of the trends identified on the company's operations in its current markets

◆ forecast the future direction of trends and examine the likely threats and opportunities presented by them

◆ evaluate the impact of the likely threats and opportunities on the company's long-term strategies.

In an early study of environmental scanning carried out by F Aguilar in 1967, four basic patterns of environmental scanning were discovered to be used by managers. These were:

1 *Undirected viewing* This was the least systematic technique and consisted of unplanned, unfocused environmental awareness.

2 *Conditioned viewing* Companies using this technique were aware of the environmental factors relevant to their activities, but environmental scanning was not carried out as an active search.

3 *Informal search* Companies using this technique collected information actively on their environments, but did so in an informal, ad hoc way.

4 *Formal search* Companies using this technique knew which environmental information was relevant to them, and employed formal methods to collect it.

Aguilar found that few companies engaged in formal environmental scanning. A later study by S C Jain in the 1980s found that more companies were engaging in environmental scanning. Jain identified typical phases through which companies went in the development of increasingly sophisticated scanning procedures. These phases are as follows:

1 *Primitive* Information is noted, but environmental scanning is largely undirected and little effort is devoted to it. No distinction is made between strategic and non-strategic information.

2 *Ad hoc* There is an increased sensitivity to environmental information, but no formal scanning procedures are adopted.

3 *Reactive* Information is collected to improve responses to markets and competition, but no formal scanning procedures are adopted.

4 *Proactive* Scanning procedures are formal and planned, the intention being to predict the environment of the future.

Environmental scanning procedures

If environmental scanning is to be effectively developed within an organisation, the implementation of procedures must have top management support. In particular, top management should establish procedures which define the following boundaries:

◆ *The micro-environment and the wider environment of the company* Precise environmental definitions are difficult to arrive at for all but the simplest business structures, but definition is necessary. Too wide a definition of the environment leads to the collection of irrelevant data; and too narrow a definition leads to relevant data being ignored.

◆ *Time limits for environmental scanning* These will vary according to the investment or product development cycle of the company. A pharmaceutical company may use a time span of up to 25 years, whereas a clothes designer may use a time span of three years or less.

◆ *Personnel responsibilities for environmental scanning activities* There are three ways in which environmental scanning can be staffed. First, line managers in sales, finance and marketing can be given responsibility for scanning in their areas of competence. This method requires line managers to receive training in scanning techniques. Second, strategic planners can be given responsibility for environmental scanning. Third, a special environmental scanning department can be established with responsibility for all scanning activities.

◆ *Formal requirements for environmental scanning activities* Some companies choose to conduct their environmental scanning informally, whereas others prefer to formalise the scanning function to a considerable degree.

The likely impact of environmental trends on a company can be assessed by planners using opportunity and threat matrices. An opportunity matrix measures environmental opportunities in terms of attractiveness and success probability. A threat matrix measures threats in terms of seriousness and occurrence probability. Figure 3.3 shows an opportunity matrix; Fig. 3.4 shows a threat matrix.

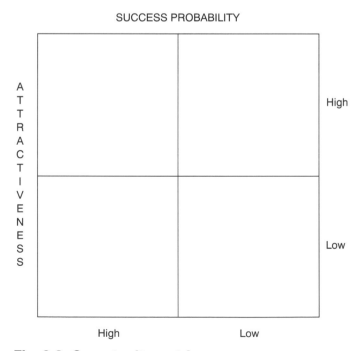

Fig. 3.3 Opportunity matrix

OCCURRENCE PROBABILITY

High

Low

High   Low

S
E
R
I
O
U
S
N
E
S
S

Fig. 3.4 Threat matrix

Marketing audits

In Chapter 14 we will look at marketing control techniques in some detail. It is enough here to give a brief description of one tool used in the control process: *the marketing audit.* A marketing audit evaluates a company's marketing objectives, policies, and procedures. Its purpose is to establish what changes need to be made by the company in order to remain effective in a changing environment. Marketing audits should be carried out on a regular basis. A marketing audit will examine both the company's external environments and its internal environment.

Factors within the macro-environment that are of importance to a marketing audit include the following:

◆ *Demographic trends* It is important to know whether changes in population levels, age distribution or density levels are likely to have an effect on business in the future. A company serving the youth market, for example, will be interested in threats or opportunities presented by changes in age distribution.

◆ *Economic trends* A company marketing consumer durables, for example, will want to know how fast the economy is growing, and how national income is distributed between different groups in society.

◆ *Politics and the law* It is important to monitor likely changes in government attitudes to business and specific legal changes. A company marketing private health care, for example, may see changes in government as posing threats or opportunities. A tobacco company will need to monitor changes in tobacco advertising law.

◆ *Technology* Technological developments are a major environmental force, and trends in product and process technology need to be monitored closely. A company which can predict and accommodate changes in technology improves its position by doing so. Forecasting technological changes is a difficult process, as the history of the domestic video-recorder shows. It took several years for the VHS/Betamax conflict to be resolved.

◆ *Social trends* Although core cultural values remain relatively stable over time, secondary values can change relatively quickly. Social trends influence not only the kinds of products that people buy or expenditure patterns, but also attitudes to the world of business.

◆ *Competitors* A company needs to identify its competitors and its competitors' strengths and weaknesses. It should monitor trends in such areas as industry structure, entry barriers and distribution systems.

◆ *Customers* Customer needs and wants may change over time, and such changes should be monitored. Some American motor-car manufacturers continued to make 'gas-guzzler' cars after the 1974 oil crisis, thus failing to spot changing customer needs and wants, which were for smaller, economic cars.

The second part of a marketing audit evaluates the marketing performance of a company. Again, its purpose is to see what changes the company should make in order to remain effective in a changing environment. An internal audit will look at such matters as marketing objectives and strategies, marketing systems and procedures, the organisation of marketing functions and their relationships with other company functions, marketing mix elements, sales, market share and profitability.

Factors that are important within the micro-environment are:

◆ the total market: size and growth rate

◆ products: leading products, product features, packaging and warranties

◆ prices: price levels, sale conditions and discounts, trade practices

◆ distribution systems: transport used, distribution channels, locations, stocks, needs and profits

- promotion: methods used, advertising, public relations and selling
- competitors: industry structure, performance levels and profitability.

Factors that are important within the internal environment are:

- company markets: market share, profitability, marketing structure and organisation
- company sales: analysis for regions, customers, segments and products
- products: product development, range and quality
- prices: levels, discounts and credit
- distribution: intermediaries
- promotion: advertising, sales promotion, selling, after-sales service and public relations.

Self-assessment test questions

These questions have been designed to test your recall of the main points in this chapter. The answers can be found on p. 219.

Complete the following sentences:

1 The basic conditions in which businesses operate are established by . . .

2 GNP by itself is not sufficient to indicate a country's business opportunities because . . .

3 Core cultural values express a society's . . .

4 Technology makes new products available and also new . . .

5 A SWOT analysis enables a company to evaluate . . .

6 A distinctive competence is an area in which . . .

7 A threat matrix measures . . .

8 An opportunity matrix measures . . .

9 The purpose of a marketing audit is to . . .

10 An internal marketing audit evaluates . . .

State whether each of the following statements is TRUE or FALSE:

11 Macro-environmental factors are within the control of the company.

12 Legislation is the principal means by which governments control business operating conditions.

13 Disposable income is calculated by subtracting from per capita income an amount for taxation plus an amount for everyday expenditure.

14 Core cultural values do not change between countries.

15 In a SWOT analysis, company weaknesses are defined in financial terms.

Write short notes to answer the following:

16 What are the four principal macro-environmental factors?

17 What is a SWOT analysis?

18 What are the functions of an external environmental scan?

19 What are the three ways in which environmental scanning activities can be staffed?

20 How are opportunity and threat matrices used in environmental scanning procedures?

 Discussion activity

The National Health Service (NHS) has changed in recent years. What are some of the macro-environmental factors which have influenced these changes? What further trends would you expect health service managers to be monitoring when they carry out environmental scanning?

4 Stakeholders

After reading this chapter you should be able to:

◆ **Define what is meant by stakeholders**

◆ **Describe the typical elements in a publicity campaign**

◆ **Identify the factors which influence supplier relationships**

◆ **Outline the chief characteristics of 'green' marketing.**

In our discussion of the micro-environment in Chapter 2 we saw P Kotler's definition of a company's publics as 'any group that has an actual or a potential interest in, or impact on, a company's ability to achieve its objectives'. Another term for such interest groups is *stakeholders*. In this chapter we will look at the relationships between a company and its various stakeholders, and the kinds of problems which can sometimes arise.

Although individual companies will have different stakeholder systems, depending on the kind of industry they are in and the size of the company, the following list indicates the extent of a typical stakeholder system:

◆ news media

◆ suppliers

◆ customers

◆ government and government departments

◆ shareholders and financial institutions

◆ employees

◆ the local community.

Its stakeholder relationships are important to a company, because the quality of these relationships has an effect on how the company is perceived in terms of its products, brand image, and general reputation. Stakeholder relationships, therefore, have to be managed, and we will look at some techniques for achieving this.

 ## Public relations

Public relations (PR) has been defined by the Institute of Public Relations as follows:

> **PR is the deliberate, planned and sustained effort to establish and maintain mutual understanding between an organisation and its publics.**

One of the functions of a public relations department is to organise company publicity. This is one of the means by which a company can seek to communicate with its publics. Publicity can be defined as a mass-media communication that is not paid for by the company. Publicity is a powerful communication tool, partly because audiences believe independent news messages from journalists more readily than they do company advertisements. The purpose of publicity is to promote the company or its products. Publicity in newspapers and on television or radio is highly valued by companies, and 'news management' is therefore one of the most important PR functions. A publicity campaign consists of the following elements:

◆ *Press releases* The company issues a short item of news to journalists. Very often press releases are published by newspapers with the minimum number of changes to the text, and so careful thought has to be given to the drafting of press releases.

◆ *Press conferences* The company invites journalists to attend a meeting at which a company announcement is made. Press conferences are used when the topic is complicated or controversial and the company wishes journalists to ask questions.

◆ *Press receptions* The company invites journalists to the unveiling of new models or new products. The journalists are encouraged to 'try out' the products for themselves.

◆ *Visits* The company invites journalists to make a tour of the factory or premises.

Media relations

Although companies are keen to receive the benefits of positive news coverage, there will always be times when press coverage is a negative or threatening experience. In 1992 Hoover received a great deal of negative publicity about a promotional offer that went badly wrong. The company had promised that purchasers of any of its products costing £100 or more would be eligible to receive two free return flights to America or Europe. When there were complaints from customers that the company was not meeting its obligations, there was a flurry of press stories in which the company received a lot of adverse criticism.

Very little can be done by companies to prevent the media from following up critical news stories. Companies can, however, make efforts to build good relations with media representatives. When bad stories break, as they will from time to time, it is wiser to co-operate and communicate than to adopt a hostile and negative stance. A company which admits its errors, and explains its plans for putting matters right, will have more successes with the news media than a company which refuses either to admit errors or to discuss them.

Supplier relations

We saw in Chapter 2 that, according to M E Porter's analysis of competitive forces, the relations of a company with its suppliers are influenced by the relative strengths of the supplier and company. In the supermarket industry, for example, independent suppliers often find themselves in a weaker position than the retail outlets which purchase their products. In other industries this position is reversed and suppliers dominate the relationship.

Suppliers and companies are both interested in building long-term relationships of mutual profitability. It is therefore important for a company to communicate its needs clearly to suppliers so that these can be met. A study by Y Wind in 1970 showed that four factors are particularly significant in explaining changes in supplier loyalty. These factors are:

1 *Economic variables* Price, quality and delivery are economic variables over which difficulties can arise when a buyer is given contradictory messages about his or her company's real requirements. The production department, for example, may stress that the quality of components is of prime importance, whereas at the same time the finance department may stress that the price of the components is of prime importance.

Where this kind of confusion occurs, company buyers are likely to choose a supplier which excels in one of the requirements and is acceptable in the other.

2 *Buyer's previous experience of suppliers* Buyers tend to make repeat purchases from known suppliers, preferring to continue in established relationships.

3 *Buyer's organisational structure* Two factors are important here. The first of these is the degree to which the products being purchased are essential to the buying company's activities. Buyers tend to be more loyal to suppliers from whom they buy essential products than they are to suppliers from whom they purchase inessential products. The second factor is the degree of risk associated with a purchase. Buyers tend to favour existing suppliers when the purchase risk is high.

4 *Factors simplifying the buyer's work* Buyers have a general tendency to remain with suppliers they know in order to simplify their work complexity.

 ## Stakeholder power analysis

Power relationships between suppliers, manufacturers and retailers have been analysed extensively in recent years. The principal sources of channel power are environmental factors such as demand, technology, and the competitive structure of the industry. Secondary power sources derive from within companies and include size, resources, experience, management and company skills. Companies perceive power in five forms:

1 *Referent power* occurs when one company wants to be associated with another because of the advantages this will bring. An independent food producer, for example, may wish to be associated with a major supermarket retailer.

2 *Expertise power* occurs when one company perceives another as having greater expertise.

3 R*eward power* occurs when one company perceives another company as being in a position to secure benefits for it.

4 *Legitimacy* occurs when one company has internalised the values of another, thus permitting the second company to exercise influence.

5 *Coercive power* occurs when one company believes that another will engage in some form of coercion if its demands are not met.

Power can be used defensively, to control the relationship between buyer and seller, by setting conditions on co-operation with the weaker party in the relationship. A strong manufacturer, for example, can demand that distributors treat its products in a specially favourable way. A strong retailer can impose a system of price discounts on a manufacturer.

As we saw in Chapter 2, one cause of conflict between suppliers and their customers is that each has separate interests. In recent years, however, there has been a growing realisation that the supplier/customer relationship can be more advantageous for both parties if a measure of co-operation and partnership is developed. These closer relationships have resulted in companies reducing the number of suppliers they deal with.

Closer relationships have resulted in changes to the traditional seller/buyer contacts between suppliers and customers. The range of these contacts has increased:

◆ supplier research and development personnel meet with customer marketing personnel

◆ supplier distribution personnel meet with customer distribution personnel.

A third effect of closer supplier/customer relationships has been the improvement of logistics systems, which are the means by which customer product needs are met. In 'quick response' logistics systems, suppliers monitor their customers' use of products and automatically replenish stocks at agreed levels. This system puts the responsibility for making product orders on the supplier rather than on the customer.

 ## Customer relations

Communicating with customers is an essential part of the marketing process, and is one of the ways to foster consumer loyalty. It is important to understand that customer loyalty takes different forms. Sometimes loyalty is to a brand; sometimes to a company; and sometimes it is to a retail outlet. Loyalty can be influenced by a number of factors other than product satisfaction, such as product price, performance, guarantees and warranties. Beyond the product itself consumer loyalty is influenced by factors such as knowledge of how the company conducts itself in a variety of other areas. Sometimes a company's business activities in other parts of the world will attract negative consumer attention. In America companies which advertise their products during the showing of violent television programmes sometimes find that customers express their disapproval by engaging in boycotts of those products.

The process towards loyalty for a typical consumer is through the five stages of what is called the *company ladder*. These stages are Suspect, Prospect, Customer, Client and Advocate (see Fig. 4.1).

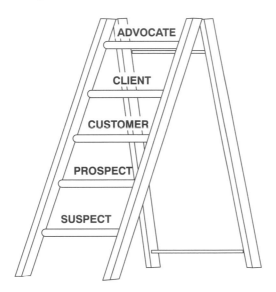

Fig. 4.1 The 'company ladder' towards customer loyalty

In the *suspect* stage, the consumer does not understand the benefits of the product or is suspicious of the company. Exposure to advertising, or recommendations from friends, may change this initial response to one of interest in the product; this is the *prospect* stage. The consumer may then decide to try the product, thus entering the third stage: that of *customer*. If the product is found to give benefits, the consumer may make a repeat purchase, thus moving from customer to *client*. The final stage in the ladder is reached when the consumer is so convinced of the product's benefits that they become an *advocate*: someone who recommends the product to others.

From the company point of view, consumer advocates are very valuable for two reasons. First, profitability is increased if a company does not have to invest heavily in attracting new customers, but can rely on a steady demand from existing companies. Second, consumer advocates are an effective source of advertising. We saw in Chapter 2 that the consumer purchase decision is influenced by recommendations from members of an individual's reference groups.

Relations with government and government departments

We saw in Chapter 3 that the government is an important environmental influence on the business world generally. With regard to particular companies, maintaining good relations with the government, or with government departments, can also be of great importance. This was essential to the consortium building the Channel Tunnel, as it is also for companies providing detention centres and prisoner escort services.

Conflict between companies and the government can arise for a number of reasons. Sometimes companies feel that ministers and their officials make laws without understanding the working methods or practices of an industry; sometimes conflict is caused by a disagreement over issues. European Union food regulations, for example, have been criticised by cheese manufacturers because, they argue, the requirements show little understanding of cheese manufacture. In the newspaper industry there has been an ongoing conflict with the government over reporting practices, particularly with regard to privacy issues.

Communication between industry and the government is maintained through a number of official and unofficial channels. It is usual for the government to request the views of interested parties before proceeding far with legislative plans, and industry experts can be called before parliamentary select committees to give their views. Constituency MPs frequently voice the concerns of local industry in the House of Commons. Additionally, there exist a number of professional and trade associations which represent the interests of industry to government. The use of these channels permits a continual negotiation between government and industry over legislative changes.

Shareholders and financial institutions

Company directors in Britain have various legal duties and responsibilities towards shareholders. Beyond such formal communications as Annual Reports and Annual General Meetings, it is important to explain company actions to investors. This can be done partly through effective media management, which will ensure press coverage in the financial sections of newspapers. Nowadays, as the number of small and relatively inexperienced investors grows, it is particularly necessary to communicate company plans to investors.

Financial institutions of importance to a company include merchant banks and other sources of loan capital. Institutions such as these will want very full details of past performance and projections of future performance, together with information about new ventures or markets.

 ## Employee relations

A very important stakeholder group is a company's own workforce. We saw in Chapter 1 that the development of a positive organisational culture is a management responsibility. In a company with a positive organisational culture, managers and employees share a common perspective about the company, its objectives, and the ways in which these objectives should be reached.

Companies use a number of techniques for building a positive company culture. These range from job-training schemes and management by objectives performance-evaluation schemes, to special team-building exercises and the formation of quality circles. The intention of all of these is to involve employees in the company so that they contribute more effectively to its operations. This is particularly important in service industries where, as we saw in Chapter 1 in the definition of 'service variability', the quality of a service depends to a great extent on the personnel who deliver it. The effective management of organisational culture is also very important in companies which are undergoing change.

 ## Local community relations

Many companies are important employers in their local communities, and wish to establish good long-term relations with the community. This can be done partly through the establishment of good industrial relations, and partly through the development of community links. Some companies have a policy of supporting local charities or sponsoring local sports or arts events. Activities like these contribute to building a positive company image in the local environment. It is also important to be sensitive to issues of local importance, such as noise pollution and care of the physical environment.

 ## Green marketing

We have said that companies need to be sensitive to stakeholder opinion and attitudes, and one area in which this is particularly true nowadays is that which concerns the physical and social environment. Consumer attitudes towards the physical environment have changed significantly in recent years. In 1991, Mintel's UK Green Consumer Survey revealed that 46 per cent of women and 31 per cent of men sought 'green' product alternatives when shopping.

It is not only consumers who are interested in environmental issues, however. Pressures for change also come from governments, the news media, pressure groups, and company employees and their representatives. A survey by Vandermerwe and Oliff in 1991 found that, within Europe, companies were responding to these stakeholder pressures by changing product offerings, production systems and marketing communications.

Green marketing is an attempt to balance company profitability against the needs of the physical and social environment. It has been defined by A Prothero in these terms:

> **Green marketing: the holistic management process responsible for identifying, anticipating, and satisfying the needs of customers and society, in a profitable and sustainable way.**

Although green marketing is related to societal marketing, a topic we shall examine in Chapter 6, it has distinct characteristics of its own,

◆ green marketing places an inherent value on the physical environment, rather than valuing it for its usefulness to business activity

◆ green marketing focuses on global concerns rather than local issues

◆ green marketing emphasises the interdependence of the economy, society and the physical environment.

The two fundamental propositions of green marketing can be stated simply. First, natural resources should not be consumed at a rate greater than that at which they can be replenished. This is known as the *concept of sustainability*. (In the case of non-renewable resources, the concept of sustainability holds that consumption should not exceed the rate at which alternative resources can be produced.) The second proposition of green marketing is that pollution and waste levels should not exceed the rate at which they can be absorbed by the environment without damage.

Central to the green marketing philosophy is the concept of *eco-performance*, by which company activity is measured against the human and natural environment. It is difficult to measure eco-performance accurately, because so many factors contribute to a company's relationship with its physical and human environment. Anita Roddick, of The Body Shop, has expressed her company's philosophy in very wide terms: 'Our products reflect our philosophy. They are formulated with care and respect. Respect for other cultures, the past, the natural world, and our customers. It's a partnership of profit and principles'.

KJ Peattie has proposed a model of green marketing. According to this model, companies need to consider the implications of a range of *external green P's* and *internal green P's*. Green marketing success is measured in terms of four *green S's* (see Fig. 4.2).

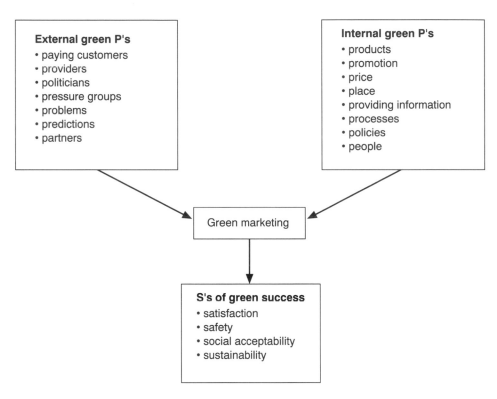

Fig. 4.2 Green marketing model

The external green P's raise the following questions and issues:

◆ *paying customers*: their level of interest, knowledge and commitment to green issues and their desire for information

◆ *providers*: their commitment to the provision of green raw materials

◆ *politicians*: activities of political lobbyists; legislative trends

◆ *pressure groups*: their current and future campaigns

◆ *problems*: the company's involvement with environmental or social problems in the past

◆ *predictions*: the company's future involvement in environmental or social problems

◆ *partners*: the company's partners' commitment to green issues.

The internal green P's raise the following questions and issues:

◆ *products*: safety and disposability; packaging

◆ *promotion*: use of green promotional messages, their substantiability and public credibility

◆ *price*: pricing for green products; willingness of customers to pay more

◆ *place*: commitment to green issues of existing distribution channel members

◆ *providing information*: business information requirements about consumers, competitors and the green agenda

◆ *processes*: green improvements to production technology

◆ *policies*: development of systems for eco-performance motivating, monitoring, evaluating and control

◆ *people*: the commitment and understanding of company personnel to the green marketing concept.

This model of green marketing recognises four S's of green marketing success. These are:

◆ *satisfaction* of customer needs

◆ *safety* of products and production for the environment, society and company employees

◆ so*cial acceptability* of all company activities

◆ *sustainability* of resources.

 # Implications of green marketing

The increasing acceptance of green marketing looks set to modify some of the traditional assumptions of marketing philosophy and practice, as companies come to terms with the need to consider the socio-environmental impact of their activities.

In Chapter 1 we quoted the Chartered Institute of Marketing's definition of marketing as 'the management process which identifies, anticipates and supplies customer requirements efficiently and profitably'. Although the green marketing approach accepts this definition of the marketing process, its emphasis on the need to consider socio-environmental issues means that the concept of customers is broadened. From a green perspective, customers no longer simply have product needs to be satisfied: they also have socio-environmental needs. Sometimes there may be conflict between these two kinds of need, and strategies will have to be formulated for balancing product needs against customers' sociocultural requirements. Increases in government taxation on fossil fuels are one way in which legislators seek to guarantee the sustainability of natural resources. In extreme circumstances it is possible that products with a poor level of eco-performance will be taken off the market. An example of this recently occurred in America, when lawn-mower manufacturers voluntarily withdrew some of their products from sale. The manufacturers did so because their products were seen as significant contributors to 'environmental noise pollution'.

Sometimes a company finds itself urged to act in contradictory ways by different stakeholders. This happened in the case of the disposal of the Royal Dutch/Shell Group's Brent Spar platform. The company had planned, with support from the government, to dump the oil rig at sea. The environmental group, Greenpeace, mounted a strong public campaign against the proposed dumping plan, arguing that the rig contained a substantial quantity of oil which would pollute the sea. Towards the end of the campaign the company found itself facing criticism from environmentalists and the news media, as well as public concern over its commitment to the physical environment. The company decided to abandon the planned dumping of the oil rig, much to the embarrassment of the government which had defended the plan vigorously. (Greenpeace later admitted that it had been mistaken when it calculated that the Brent Spar contained 5500 tons of oil. Greenpeace apologised to the company but insisted that it had been right to oppose the plan.)

Self-assessment test questions

These questions have been designed to test your recall of the main points in this chapter. The answers can be found on p. 219.

Complete the following sentences:

1 Stakeholder relationships affect perceptions of a company in terms of its . . .

2 The purpose of publicity is to . . .

3 Suppliers and companies are both interested in building . . .

4 Consumer loyalty can be focused on three variables. These are . . .

5 The five stages of the company ladder are . . .

6 Companies support local charities and events in order to . . .

7 Green marketing is an attempt to balance company profitability against . . .

8 The principle of sustainability means that . . .

9 The four S's of green marketing success are . . .

10 Green marketing suggests that customers not only have product needs to be satisfied, but that they also have . . .

State whether each of the following statements is TRUE or FALSE:

11 The purpose of a press reception is to discuss a complex matter with journalists.

12 In quick-response logistics systems the supplier makes product orders.

13 A product advocate is a legal representative.

14 Green marketing focuses on global concerns rather than local issues.

15 Vandermerwe and Oliff found that green marketing is not of much interest to European companies.

Write short notes on the following:

16 public relations

17 media relations

18 consumer relations

19 government relations

20 green marketing.

Group activity

A local entrepreneur has applied for planning permission to build a large night-club in your town. The planning authorities have received a number of letters about the project from members of the public and from local organisations. Some of these letters were favourable to the idea and some were not.

Working together, try to draw up a list of stakeholders and estimate whether they would be in favour of the nightclub or not. What arguments might the entrepreneur use with different stakeholders to persuade them to support his project?

Marketing for services and non-profit organisations

After reading this chapter you should be able to:

◆ Describe the four ways in which services differ from conventional products

◆ List the five factors influencing customer service expectations

◆ Explain why non-profit organisations may have ambiguous goals

◆ Explain why it can be difficult to identify customers for non-profit organisations

◆ Distinguish between the barrier approach and the facilitator approach to funding.

Britain's economy is a service economy, which means that more wealth is produced, and more people are employed, in services than in manufacturing. The service sector consists of various non-profit-making government services, such as education, health, the justice system, and the armed forces. It also consists of privately-owned businesses, such as the financial services industry, professional services, and the leisure and entertainment industries.

Before we consider how the marketing of services differs from the marketing of other products, it is important to distinguish exactly what is meant by services. In Chapter 1 we saw that services are different to products in four important ways. These are:

1 *Intangibility* It is impossible to see, touch, taste, smell or hear most services before purchasing them. Some services are more intangible than

others: a solicitor's advice is more intangible than a hotel bedroom, for example, but in both cases the purchaser of the service does not receive permanent evidence of a service.

The intangibility of services creates special problems for companies to overcome. First, it is difficult for potential customers to judge the value of a service which they have not purchased before, partly because services cannot be purchased in small, 'test' amounts. It is therefore necessary for companies to stress the tangible elements in the service environment, and to explain the service in terms of customer value. High-street opticians do this when they provide attractive premises and literature which sets out the benefits of having regular eye-sight tests.

2 *Inseparability* With conventional products, the making of the product and its sale precede consumption. With services, however, the making of the service and its consumption frequently occur at the same time. An example of this kind of inseparability is a 'live' musical performance, which is produced and consumed at the same time. Obviously musicians practise their performance before going on stage, but on the night of a concert they are producing their service in front of the audience.

3 *Perishability* A service, such as a musical performance, cannot be stored.

4 *Variability* The inseparability of services means that it is difficult to standardise them. A group of musicians may give a brilliant performance one night, for example, but for some reason their next performance of the same piece of music may not be quite as good. Service quality depends on the personnel who deliver it, much more so than with conventional products. A rude shop assistant may make the purchasing of a television set an unpleasant experience, but will not affect the ultimate enjoyment of the product. An unhelpful tour guide, however, can ruin enjoyment of the whole service.

The fast-food chains, like McDonald's, have gone a long way towards providing standardised services, by developing procedures and working practices which result in a very similar experience in any outlet.

We saw in Chapter 1 that the marketing mix for products consists of the four P's: product, price, promotion and place. Many analysts have suggested that additional elements should be added to these basic four, and there is a growing acceptance of the idea that a fifth P deserves a place:

people. It is now recognised that whether a company is engaged in the marketing of conventional products or of services, the behaviour of its staff towards customers can be a crucial factor in competitive performance.

The addition of 'people' to the services marketing mix is justified because, as we have seen, variability means that the quality of a service depends on the personnel who deliver it. The marketing mix for services is illustrated in Fig. 5.1. Note the term *tangible cues* in the Product element. Tangible cues are physical indications of service quality. These are necessary because of the intangible nature of services. Tangible cues include the physical environment in which the service takes place, for example, the decor of a hotel. Figure 5.2 shows G L Shostack's representation of tangibility and intangibility in goods and services.

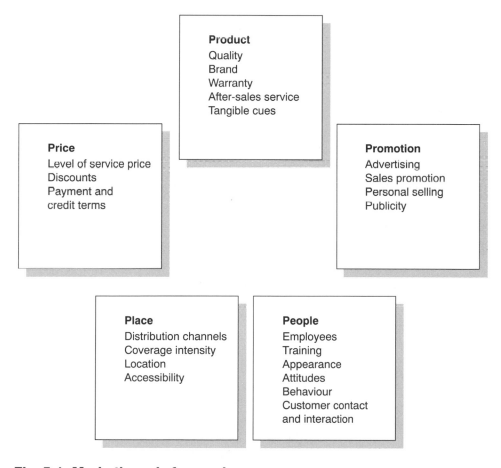

Product
Quality
Brand
Warranty
After-sales service
Tangible cues

Price
Level of service price
Discounts
Payment and
credit terms

Promotion
Advertising
Sales promotion
Personal selling
Publicity

Place
Distribution channels
Coverage intensity
Location
Accessibility

People
Employees
Training
Appearance
Attitudes
Behaviour
Customer contact
and interaction

Fig. 5.1 Marketing mix for services

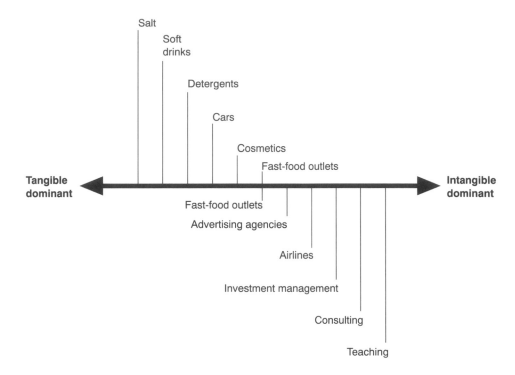

Fig. 5.2 Tangibility and intangibility of goods and services

Some critics have argued that it is not necessary to modify the marketing mix for services. T Levitt, for example, denies the existence of services as a separate entity:

> There is no such thing as service industries. There are only industries whose service components are greater or lesser than other industries. Everybody is in service.

 Service quality

It is more difficult for customers to evaluate services than conventional products, and for this reason companies are likely to give a lot of thought to the physical environment in which the service is delivered, or where this is inappropriate, to the creation of a service image, and tangible features. Typical tangible service features include advertising and promotional literature.

Service quality is focused on satisfying customers' needs, and in that sense does not differ from product quality, which is also focused on the satisfaction of customer needs. With a service, however, it is sometimes difficult to gauge customer expectations. One way of doing this concentrates on five factors influencing expectations. These are:

1 *Tangibles*. These are aspects in the physical environment.

2 *Reliability*. This refers to the organisation's ability to deliver the service dependably, accurately and consistently.

3 *Responsiveness*. This refers to the organisation's ability to deliver the service promptly and helpfully.

4 *Assurance*. This refers to the organisation's ability to deliver the service in a way that makes customers confident.

5 *Empathy*. This refers to the organisation's ability to deliver the service in a way that shows understanding of the needs of individual customers.

The development of a quality service plan rests on first identifying the needs of customers. Once these have been determined, service production and delivery can be centred around them. It is important that company personnel receive training which describes company service objectives, and teaches ways of achieving them. The development of an appropriate organisational culture is of great importance to service organisations.

An effective quality service plan also allows for the periodic assessment of quality performance, and systems for resolving quality problems when these arise.

 ## Marketing and non-profit organisations

There are many organisations in a modern society whose primary purpose is not to make a profit, but to further some non-commercial aim. Some of these organisations have legal charitable status, and others do not. Although non-profit organisations do not come into existence in order to make profits, they frequently engage in money-making activities in order to reach their objectives: and for this reason it is worth considering how far such organisations could make use of the marketing concept.

Non-profit organisations differ from conventional business organisations in several significant respects. First, because their purpose is not primarily commercial, they may have ambiguous goals. An example of this might be a charity organisation working in the field of AIDS. Typically, such an organisation would consist of a board of trustees with certain legal responsibilities, employees and voluntary workers. Individuals within each of these three groups may have strong, and different, views about the fundamental objectives of the organisation. The trustees, for example, might stress the need for raising public awareness about AIDS-related issues; they might also wish the organisation to become involved in medical research. Employees, however, might wish the organisation to concentrate its efforts on the provision of medical treatment rather than research, arguing that this is of greater practical benefit to sufferers. The volunteers might put more emphasis on the need to 'de-stigmatise' AIDS and AIDS sufferers.

Second, even where there is agreement about fundamental objectives, there may be considerable disagreement about how the objectives are to be reached, particularly when decisions about spending and raising money have to be made.

A third difference between non-profit organisations and conventional business organisations is that it is difficult to measure the outputs of a non-profit organisation. A business organisation's outputs can be measured in terms of profit. If levels of profit indicate the extent of a business's success, what criteria could be adopted as measures of success of an AIDS charity, such as the one previously described? Many non-profit organisations attempt to overcome this problem by measuring inputs rather than outputs. Inputs for an AIDS charity might be the number of publicity campaigns organised in a year and the number of people counselled in a year. These inputs give an indication of how active an organisation is, but they do not indicate how far these activities have furthered the charity's objectives.

 ## Defining customers for non-profit organisations

Sometimes it is difficult to know how to define the customers of a non-profit organisation. Consider, for example, the case of a private hostel dealing with homeless people. At first sight it might seem that the homeless people themselves are the organisation's customers. Although the homeless people are not paying for the service, they are certainly receiving it. From the point of view of payment, however, it would be correct to say that the local authority, which funds the hostel, is a customer. In the same sense that the local authority is a customer, the individuals who donate money to the hostel can also be perceived as customers.

Many non-profit organisations receive their funding from local and central government sources, and therefore have to negotiate in the same way that business organisations do. This involves trying to put a price on the service being provided, and two approaches to this have been developed.

The barrier approach

Some charities argue that their role is to act as a barrier between the vulnerable and normal market forces. This used to be the stance taken by charities representing the interests of people with severe learning difficulties. A non-profit organisation with this approach can make an estimate of the costs of its service provision, and use this as the basis for negotiations with funders.

The facilitator approach

Some charities argue that their role is to rehabilitate vulnerable people, who can then take an active place in society once more. A non-profit organisation with this approach can estimate the costs to society of not providing their service, and then the costs of rehabilitation. An organisation dealing with alcohol abuse, for example, might estimate that an untreated alcoholic will cost X pounds per year in unemployment benefits and medical care, whereas therapy and rehabilitation might cost 80 per cent of this.

The marketing mix for non-profit organisations

In Chapter 1 we saw that the marketing mix for conventional businesses consists of four elements: product, price, promotion and place. It is worth considering how these elements apply to non-profit organisations.

Non-profit organisations seek to obtain non-commercial responses from their markets. Despite this difference between non-profit organisations and conventional businesses, P Kotler has argued that the concept of exchange relationships is still relevant, as in the following examples:

◆ The police have a marketing objective to serve and protect the public by enforcing the law. In return they wish to receive payment, co-operation and support.

◆ The church has a marketing objective to inform the public about its doctrines and to convince people to join. In return it wishes to receive contributions, services and an acceptance of its values.

◆ A typical charity has a marketing objective to serve the needs and wants of clients and the donor public. In return it wishes to receive contributions, time and support.

It can be seen from these examples that non-profit organisations are more concerned with the marketing of services and ideas than with traditional products. It is therefore essential that such organisations define their objectives clearly, so that they can communicate the benefits of their activities to the market. When the Marriage Guidance Council changed its name to Relate, this signalled an important aspect of its product: that the organisation offers relationship counselling and not just counselling for married couples.

Regarding the second element of the marketing mix, price, we have already seen that charity organisations are forced, when applying for funding, to put a monetary value on their activities.

Promotion is the third element in the marketing mix, and it is here that non-profit organisations can perhaps learn most from traditional marketing techniques. Non-profit organisations use a variety of promotional methods, from advertising and publicity to the arrangement of special events, competitions or entertainments.

Place is the final element of the marketing mix. Non-profit organisations need to consider how they distribute their product, service or ideas. The product must be available to the market, whether this means opening offices where a service can take place, as in the case of Relate or the Samaritans; or using media to communicate ideas, as in the case of Greenpeace or Liberty.

 ## Marketing control for non-profit organisations

As with conventional business organisations, non-profit organisations need to undertake regular audits of their marketing activities. Budgetary control techniques can be used to measure financial performance, and other techniques used for evaluating how effectively the fundamental objectives of the organisation are being met. A housing charity, seeking to provide accommodation for people with mental health problems, may supplement traditional budgetary controls with questionnaires and surveys of its client group to evaluate how effectively it is achieving its aims.

Self-assessment test questions

These questions have been designed to test your recall of the main points in this chapter. The answers can be found on p. 220.

Complete the following sentences:

1 The characteristics which make services different to conventional products are . . .

2 The addition of the element 'people' to the services marketing mix is justified because . . .

3 Service tangibles are . . .

4 Service reliability refers to an organisation's ability to . . .

5 Service responsiveness refers to an organisation's ability to . . .

6 Service assurance refers to an organisation's ability to . . .

7 Service empathy refers to an organisation's ability to . . .

8 Non-profit organisations may have ambiguous goals because . . .

9 The barrier approach to funding works by . . .

10 The facilitator approach to funding works by . . .

State whether each of the following statements is TRUE or FALSE:

11 The service sector of the economy is made up of non-profit organisations.

12 Tangible cues are physical indications of service quality.

13 T Levitt has argued that service industries do not really exist.

14 Non-profit organisations seek non-commercial responses from their markets.

15 Non-profit organisations are sometimes involved in the marketing of ideas.

Write short notes on the following:

16 intangibility, inseparability, perishability and variability

17 the marketing mix for services

18 gauging customer expectations for services

19 the differences between non-profit organisations and conventional businesses

20 the marketing mix for non-profit organisations.

 Group activity

You have been asked by the church in your area to assist in a special fund-raising campaign. The purpose of the campaign is to raise money to restore the 'historical manuscripts' section of the church library, which was damaged by fire three months ago. The local authority has promised that it will match, pound for pound, contributions from the public.

How would you approach this task, and what special difficulties would you predict in persuading people to donate money to this campaign?

Social responsibilities

After reading this chapter you should be able to:

◆ **Explain what is meant by consumerism**

◆ **List the consumer rights outlined by President Kennedy**

◆ **Describe what is meant by 'societal marketing'**

◆ **Distinguish between open and proprietary product standards**

◆ **Describe how television and radio advertising are controlled**

◆ **Describe the functions of the Advertising Standards Authority.**

 ## Consumerism

We saw in Chapter 1 that the marketing concept is based on exchange relationships. In theory, both parties in an exchange relationship have the same measure of freedom to enter or leave the relationship. In practice, however, the balance of strength between an individual consumer and a large business organisation is sometimes uneven. A business organisation has greater resources than any individual customer, and this has led sometimes to companies abusing the trust on which exchange relationships depend. In America in the 1960s, Vance Packard, Ralph Nader and others exposed some of these abuses, focusing on issues such as environmental pollution, the over-exploitation of natural resources, ethical standards in advertising, and poor standards of product quality and safety. Their criticisms led to the founding of consumer groups whose functions were to restore the balance of power between individual consumers and business organisations. This became known as *consumerism*.

In Britain the move towards consumerism has been slower, although in recent years it has received support from the government, which has published various Citizens' Charters for users of state-run industries or government departments. Some of the best-known consumer groups in Britain are:

◆ 'Which?' magazine, which publishes a wealth of product information and carries out product tests

◆ local government Trading Standards departments, which offer advice to consumers on a range of issues.

Although there is no generally agreed definition of consumerism, the consumer movement can be understood as a partnership between pressure groups, consumer associations and governments, to protect the interests of consumers. In 1962 President Kennedy outlined the American government's role in the consumerist movement by reference to four consumer 'rights'. These are:

1 *The right to safety* It may seem that consumers have an obvious right to expect that the products they buy should be safe, but the right to safety has involved companies in complicated legal and moral conflicts, particularly in America.

Such conflicts can arise when advances in knowledge mean that a product previously regarded as safe is shown to be dangerous. Cigarettes, for example, are now generally regarded as 'unsafe' products because of the established link between smoking and cancer. Does this mean that cancer victims should be able to sue cigarette companies for the damage caused to their health before the risks of smoking were widely known? Is it enough for tobacco companies, now that the risks are well known, simply to print health warnings on their packaging, or should they be obliged to do more?

Sometimes advances in knowledge are contradictory. The National Health Service advises the British public on 'safe' levels of alcohol intake, while at the same time other research seems to indicate that a moderate intake of alcohol may have beneficial health effects. During the 1970s many consumers reduced their butter consumption in favour of margarine products, which were thought to be healthier. Research now seems to indicate that certain polyunsaturates in margarines may contain risks of their own.

Conflicts also arise over product safety when consumers misuse products or suffer injury even when the product is not faulty. In a famous case in America, a lady successfully sued a fast-food restaurant which had sold her a cup of coffee that she claimed was dangerously hot. She had been badly injured when the coffee spilled onto her lap while she was driving. To what extent should product safety depend on the consumer's use of a product?

2 *The right to be informed* Most countries now have laws which require companies to give consumers accurate and true product and price information, to list product ingredients, and to provide accurate product operating instructions on dangerous or complex equipment. There have been problems in the past with company advertisements for timeshare apartments, and diet plans and foods, as well as beauty products whose manufacturers have made extravagant claims about their ability to slow the ageing process.

3 *The right to choose* Product choice depends on the provision of accurate information. Information should be presented in such a way that consumers can tell the difference between similar products.

4 *The right to be heard* As consumer confidence grows, there is an increasing tendency for consumers to express their views to business organisations. The right to be heard has been interpreted as including not only such matters as customer complaints about poor products and services, but more general issues as well. In America it is becoming increasingly common for consumers to express their dissatisfaction with companies' overseas investment, employment policies, or environmental performance, through product boycotts.

Although consumerism sometimes expresses itself aggressively, as in the example of product boycotts, the consumerist movement generally should not be seen as a threat by companies with a genuine marketing orientation. Rather, consumerism offers companies an opportunity to listen to their customers, to understand their needs more fully, and thus to respond to them more completely.

 ## Societal marketing

In his book 'Marketing Management' (4th edn, Prentice-Hall, 1980), P Kotler suggests that marketing is about more than the simple fulfilment of customer needs in terms of products. In Kotler's view, a company should consider how its activities affect the social, business and physical environment of which it is a part. According to this *societal marketing* concept, the satisfaction of customer needs remains the principal function of marketing professionals, but with the proviso that customer needs should not be satisfied at the expense of the physical environment, or the long-term interests of consumers themselves.

The implications of the societal marketing concept are that there are circumstances in which a company may either withdraw a product, change its method of manufacture, or refuse to sell it to certain categories of customer. A retailer who follows the societal marketing concept may refuse to sell a glue product to a potential customer, if it is believed that the customer is a substance abuser.

 ## Cause marketing

The concept of social responsibility in marketing has led to what is called *cause marketing*. Cause marketing takes two forms. The first is when a company identifies itself with a cause of some kind, usually making a connection between its main business activity and the cause which it is espousing. The Body Shop, for example, campaigns for environmental and third world causes, as well as donating money to HIV awareness programmes for women. The cosmetics company Avon funds breast cancer research. The link between The Body Shop's and Avon's business activities and their causes is clear. Sometimes, however, a company will try to make a link between itself and a cause without there being any obvious connection from the point of view of the company's business activity. The clothes store Benetton, for example, is famous for its controversial series of billboard advertisements which have featured AIDS issues, racial prejudice and religious symbols, all carrying the slogan 'United Colors of Benetton'. Benetton advertisements have caused offence to some people, who have dismissed its billboard themes as exploitative. The company, however, defends itself from charges of exploitation by insisting that its commitment to causes is genuine.

It seems likely that cause marketing will increase in the future, as companies work harder to please their stakeholder groups. It is also likely that the proportion of cause marketing associated with environmental issues will increase, because environmental protection issues are among the least contentious causes a company can adopt.

 ## Ethical issues in marketing

Ethics can be defined as the social and moral standards which are acceptable to a given society. For marketing purposes, ethical issues involve matters such as employment practices, pricing policies, product quality and safety, advertising and promotion, and care of the environment. As we have seen, a lot of these matters are covered by specific pieces of legislation, but there is still a need for companies to formulate precise ethical strategies for the guidance of their employees.

Ethical issues arise particularly in the international marketing environment, where cultural differences create ambiguity. Questions that need to be considered include the following: Is it correct to make, or receive, gifts when negotiating contracts? Should all such gifts be formally recorded, or only gifts above a certain value?

US FIRMS LOST BUSINESS DUE TO BRIBES, REPORT SAYS

Since last year, foreign companies used bribes to edge out US competitors on some $45 billion of international business deals, according to a classified report that US Commerce Secretary Ron Brown is expected to present to Congress today.

The report, assembled with the help of US intelligence agencies, contains hundreds of examples of bribery as well as legitimate, often government-assisted, export promotion. The study was conducted to gauge the intensity of competition US companies face abroad and to try to develop policy responses, US officials said.

The report also marks a turning point for US intelligence agencies as they search for a new role in the post-Cold War world. US President Bill Clinton and his administration have put a high priority on having US intelligence agencies monitor misdeeds by US business's competitors.

Nonetheless, the intelligence agencies insist information about bribes or other illicit activities by foreign companies is used only to put diplomatic pressure on foreign governments to stop the unfair competition. The Central Intelligence Agency has said it won't spy for the benefit of US firms. 'We do not do industrial espionage,' John Deutch, the director of Central Intelligence, asserted in an August interview.

In a recent speech CIA Inspector General Frederick Hitz said the agency could play an important role in 'leveling the playing field for our companies doing business abroad'. He mentioned the development of counter-intelligence programs to help in preventing foreign intelligence services from penetrating US companies.

The Wall Street Journal Europe,
October 12 1995

D P Robin and R E Reidenbach have argued that marketing involves two kinds of ethical questions: macro-ethical marketing questions refer to the fundamental functions of marketing; and micro-ethical marketing questions refer to the specific actions of companies. In their view, a company's marketing function is judged to be ethical in the macro-ethical sense by reference to the following factors:

- marketing history
- social period
- context

- expectations of society
- requirements of capitalism
- understanding of human behaviour.

Product quality and standards

Product standards are important because purchasers need to be certain when they buy a component that it has the characteristics they expect and require. Standards are the result of technical specifications, which may vary from country to country. There is currently a movement towards the development of uniform standards, to make international trade easier. Standards are said to be *proprietary* if they are the work of a single company, such as the Microsoft 'Windows' programs. Standards are said to be *open* if they are arrived at by agreement between competitors within an industry. When standards are open, customer choice is extended because competitors provide a range of alternative products, according to the prevailing standard.

ADOPTION OF PRODUCT STANDARD

Twelve major technology and photography companies, including Motorola Inc and Eastman Kodak Co, today will unveil an agreement to adopt a match-book size memory cartridge as the standard for products including digital cameras, computers and pagers.

The CompactFlash cartridge, developed and introduced last year by San Disk Corp in California, can store images, text and voice data. By making the cartridge compatible with their individual products, the companies hope to smooth the transmission of pictures and data between different devices such as cameras, computers, printers, pagers and cellular phones.

The CompactFlash Association will make available technical specifications of the cartridges as well as the CompactFlash trademark under a royalty-free licence. Other companies can become voting members of the group and access the information for $5000.

The Wall Street Journal Europe,
October 11 1995

Within the European Union (EU) a Council of Ministers directive has been introduced which is designed to bring member states' laws into harmony on the issue of industrial product standards. The directive makes it easier for consumers to bring legal actions for compensation for faulty products.

Where previously a customer buying a defective product had to prove that a manufacturer or producer had been negligent, the new directive now places the burden of proof on the manufacturer or producer. The directive covers not only product defects, but also design defects and product warnings. A manufacturer of a product who does not warn customers of the product risks can be liable for damages under the directive.

The liability for defects extends from the retailer, through the intermediaries, to the manufacturer. Each channel member must be able to demonstrate that the responsibility for the product defect does not lie with them. If a channel member is unable to identify the source of a product, liability rests with that channel member. If a product was imported into the EU, the importing company is treated as the manufacturer or producer of the product.

Linked to the issue of product standards, which define the technical specifications of products and their components, is the issue of quality. The pursuit of quality, in both manufacturing and service industries, has led to the European adoption of the ISO 9000 quality assurance system. To qualify for ISO 9000 recognition, a company has to demonstrate that it has an effective, documented system for managing and developing its quality assurance. The ISO 9000 series has six standards:

◆ ISO 9000 is a series of quality assurance guidelines available for companies.

◆ ISO 9001 (model 1) is a model for quality assurance applicable to companies involved in product design and development, production, installation and service. It is the most demanding of the ISO 9000 series because of the range of activities covered.

◆ ISO 9002 (model 2) is a model for quality assurance applicable to companies involved in production and installation. It is used by companies whose manufacturing is carried out according to established designs.

◆ ISO 9003 (model 3) is a model for quality assurance in the final inspection and testing of manufactured products.

◆ ISO 9004 provides guidelines for quality management.

◆ ISO 9004 part 2 provides guidelines for quality management in service industries.

Controls on marketing

With regard to specific marketing activities, such as advertising and promotion, company activity is controlled either by legislation or by statutory authority, or by self-regulation. We will look at each of these control mechanisms in turn.

As we saw in Chapter 3's discussion of the macro-environmental factors which influence marketing, specific pieces of legislation have been drawn up to control competition and monopolies, and to protect the interests of consumers. The most important of these include:

◆ The Fair Trading Act, 1973

◆ The Trades Descriptions Act, 1973

◆ The Consumer Credit Act, 1974

◆ The Unfair Contract Terms Act, 1977

◆ The Sale of Goods Act, 1979.

The 1990 Broadcasting Act placed control of television advertising in the hands of a statutory body called the Independent Television Commission (ITC). The Commission regulates television advertising by reference to its Code of Advertising Standards and Practice, and its Code of Programme Sponsorship.

The ITC requires that television advertising should be 'legal, decent, honest and truthful'. There are special parts of the Code covering such matters as:

◆ advertisements directed at children

◆ financial advertising

◆ health product advertising

◆ charitable and religious advertising.

All television advertisements must be submitted to the Broadcast Advertising Clearance Centre before they are transmitted.

Complaints about television advertisements are investigated by the Independent Television Commission. During the course of its investigations, the advertisement under question is withdrawn. Every month the ITC publishes a Television Advertising Complaints Report, which details its work in the investigation of advertisement complaints. About 3000 such complaints are investigated each year.

The Broadcasting Act of 1990 also established a Radio Authority, which has its own Code of Advertising Standards and Practice and Programme Sponsorship. The Radio Authority's Code is similar to that of the ITC, with its insistence that radio advertising be 'legal, decent, honest and truthful'. There are special parts of the Code covering such matters as:

◆ advertisements directed at children

◆ financial advertising

◆ health product advertising

◆ charitable and religious advertising.

Unlike television advertisements, not all radio advertisements have to be cleared before transmission. Local and regional advertisements can be cleared by the stations transmitting them, provided they do not deal with any of the following topics:

◆ finance or consumer credit

◆ political, industrial or commercial controversy

◆ health matters

◆ environmental matters

◆ charities or religions.

Advertisements dealing with these subjects have to be submitted to the Broadcast Advertising Clearance Centre, as do all advertisements for a national audience.

Non-broadcast advertisements are subject to control by the Advertising Standards Authority (ASA), the self-regulatory body established by the industry's Advertising Association. The tasks of the Advertising Standards Authority are to investigate complaints from the public about advertisements, and to publicise its system of advertising control. The ASA works according to The British Code of Advertising Standards.

Non-broadcast advertisements are not subject to control before publication, and the ASA is only empowered to investigate an advertisement after receiving a complaint, of which there are about 8000 annually. If the Authority finds that a complaint against an advertiser is justified, it requests the advertiser to withdraw the offending advertisement. Most advertisers comply with such a request, because the Authority has a number of sanctions it can apply in the case of non-compliance. These include:

◆ requesting media owners to deny the advertiser use of their facilities in future

◆ requesting media owners to accept no further advertisements from that source if they have not been cleared by the Authority.

The Advertising Standards Authority also has a regulatory role in sales promotions through its British Code of Sales Promotions Practice. The ASA has a further Code of Practice on the Use of Personal Data for Advertising.

The Direct Marketing Association regulates direct marketing operations through its Code of Practice, which seeks, among other objectives, to 'respect the reasonable privacy and personal taste of consumers'.

 ## Self-assessment test questions

These questions have been designed to test your recall of the main points in this chapter. The answers can be found on p. 220.

Complete the following sentences:

1 The four consumer rights outlined by President Kennedy are . . .

2 According to the societal marketing concept, the satisfaction of customer needs should not be at the expense of . . .

3 Ethics can be defined as . . .

4 Standards are proprietary when . . .

5 To qualify for ISO 9000 recognition, a company has to . . .

6 The control of television advertising is carried out by a statutory body called . . .

7 All television advertisements must be submitted for approval to . . .

8 Non-broadcast advertisements are subject to control through the . . .

9 The regulatory body for sales promotions is the . . .

10 The regulatory body for direct marketing is the . . .

State whether each of the following statements is TRUE or FALSE:

11 The consumer movement is a partnership between pressure groups, consumer associations and governments.

12 Marketing ethics are fully covered by specific pieces of legislation.

13 Product standards are open when they are the work of a single company.

14 The ISO 9000 series has six standards.

15 Radio advertisements for a national audience do not have to be cleared before transmission.

Write short notes on the following:

16 the consumer movement

17 consumer rights

18 societal marketing

19 statutory controls on marketing

20 regulatory controls on marketing.

Group activity

Using the four consumer rights described by President Kennedy, work together to prepare a list of specific rights for the following customer groups:

◆ computer buyers

◆ airline passengers

◆ students

◆ solicitors' clients.

What problems would you have in implementing any of the rights which you have identified? Is it more difficult to define consumer rights for students and solicitors' clients than for computer buyers and airline passengers?

Competitive position

After reading this chapter you should be able to:

◆ **Explain what is meant by market size, market share and market growth**

◆ **Describe the characteristics of the BCG matrix and the GE business screen**

◆ **Distinguish between direct, close and indirect competition**

◆ **Distinguish between the three strategies for success identified by M E Porter.**

In previous chapters we have stressed that the marketing orientation begins and ends with customer satisfaction. Modern business conditions dictate that companies should also develop market and competitor orientations if they are to thrive. It is these orientations that we will examine in this chapter. First we will look at what is meant by market size and market share analysis. Then we will consider how to identify competitors, how to evaluate their objectives and strategies, their strengths and weaknesses, and how to predict their behaviour. In the second part of the chapter we will examine the contribution of industry structure to company profitability, and look at three strategies for success that have been identified. Finally, we will describe some offensive and defensive strategies that have been developed from comparing the business environment with the military environment.

 ## Market size

In Chapter 1 we said that a market is made up of the buyers of a product. An estimation of market size is therefore an estimation of how many buyers there are in a total market. We saw in Chapter 2 that it is important for a company to define its market with care before moving on to estimate market size, because an estimation of market size is partly dependent on the market definition used. The example given previously from T Levitt illustrates this point. In Levitt's opinion, American film-makers defined their market solely in terms of their product offerings. This market definition meant that they were not concerned by the development of television, because television was seen as a separate product, and there-fore a separate market. Had the film-makers defined themselves as being in the business of satisfying entertainment needs, however, they would have seen the development of television as a worrying new arrival in their market.

For most markets an estimate of total market size is easily obtainable from published sources of market data. These are discussed further in Chapter 8. For industrial markets, however, and markets in less-developed countries, obtaining published data on market sizes may be more difficult.

As well as knowing how many actual buyers there are, a company will want to estimate the number of potential buyers. The gap between the actual market size for cellular phones, for example, and the potential mar-ket size, is quite large. Market growth is an estimation of how quickly market size will expand to reach its estimated potential.

So far we have spoken of markets as if there were no important differences between buyers. This is not the case. Markets are made up of people with different needs, family and social backgrounds, occupations, and incomes. Total markets are divided into groups of people with different product needs. These groups are known as *market segments*. A company should determine which market segments it wishes to serve and should estimate their sizes. (Market segmentation is discussed in Chapter 15.)

 ## Market share

The purpose of market share analysis is to determine how well a company is performing within the total market and how well it is doing against its most important competitors. There are several ways of measuring market share, as Figs. 7.1–7.3 show.

In Fig. 7.1 market share is expressed by volume; in Fig. 7.2 market share is expressed by value; and in Fig. 7.3 a company's major competitor's market share is shown.

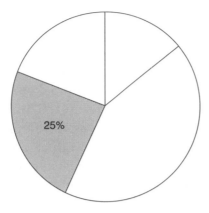

Fig. 7.1 Share of total market by volume

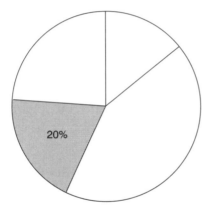

Fig. 7.2 Share of total market by value

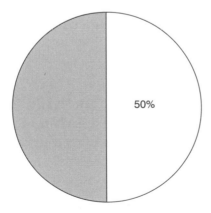

Fig. 7.3 Share of largest competitor

Care has to be taken when interpreting market share. Sometimes a change in market share is the result of company action, and sometimes it is the result of a change in the market. Markets do not remain static. All the time new products are being launched, recently-launched products are reaching their growth potentials, and the demand for older products is levelling out or declining. This process is called the *product life-cycle* (see Fig. 7.4). Market share analysis should take into account where products are in their life-cycle.

The product life-cycle

The product life-cycle concept suggests that all products go through a cycle of four phases: Introduction, Growth, Maturity and Decline. This cycle is illustrated in its most typical form in Fig. 7.4. It is important to note that, for different products, values along the horizontal (*time*) axis and the vertical (*sales*) axis, are not the same.

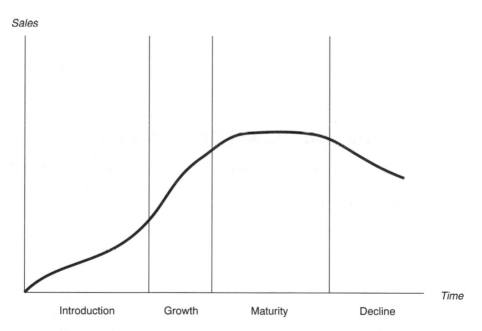

Fig. 7.4 Product life-cycle

1 *Introduction phase* The product is launched onto the market. Profits are liable to be small, or non-existent if the product has undergone a long period of research and development, as in the case of the pharmaceutical industry.

2 *Growth phase* If the new product survives the introduction phase, this is followed by a period in which it attracts more customers. As sales increase, competitors may enter the market with improved versions of the product.

3 *Maturity* During this phase, sales grow until they reach their peak and begin to decline. Declining demand can be attributable to a number of factors: the market is saturated, customers have become bored with the product, or new products have entered the market.

4 *Decline* During this phase, demand for the product falls away, and the company must decide whether to continue with a product whose profits are falling, or to withdraw it from the market.

P Kotler has argued that there are three levels of product life-cycle. The first of these is the *product category* life-cycle. An example of a product category is the generic product 'bread'. Product category life-cycles are considerably extended in time, and may show no evidence of decline. Next is the *product form* life-cycle. An example of a product form is 'sliced bread'. Product form life-cycles are shorter than product category life-cycles. Finally, there is the *product brand* life-cycle. An example of a product brand is 'Allinson's wholemeal sliced bread'. Product brand life-cycles are the shortest of the three.

The Boston Consulting Group matrix

In the 1960s the Boston Consulting Group (BCG) devised a growth/share matrix by which companies can formulate their product strategies. The matrix is shown in Fig. 7.5.

The BCG matrix classifies products into four types, according to the two variables of market growth and market share. The four product types have a connection with the phases of the product life-cycle.

1 *Problem children* are products with a low current market share but with a high growth potential. These products consume company resources during this phase. Some problem children will go on to become stars, and others will fail. (*Introduction phase of the product life-cycle.*)

2 *Stars* are successfully-managed problem children which have achieved a high current market share and still have growth potential. These products consume promotional resources, as the company seeks to maintain their market share. (*Growth phase of the product life-cycle.*)

Stars	**Problem children**
Cash cows	**Dogs**

Fig. 7.5 Boston Consulting Group portfolio matrix

3 *Cash cows* are stars which have achieved their full growth potential and now generate income for the company, which can be invested in the development of more problem children. (*Maturity phase of the product life-cycle.*)

4 *Dogs* are products in decline. They have low growth potential and low market share. (*Decline phase of the product life-cycle.*)

The BCG matrix encourages companies to maintain a balanced portfolio of products in order to preserve a positive net cash flow. Although it is a popular and useful tool, the BCG matrix has certain limitations. First, it concentrates on only two market dimensions: market growth and market share. Second, not all products are designed to become market leaders, and there is therefore some doubt as to whether performance evaluation should be linked to relative market share. We shall see later in this chapter that some companies deliberately follow a 'niche' strategy, in which the intention is to achieve profitability while remaining small in terms of market share. Third, the matrix relies on cash flow as a performance criterion, when many analysts think return on investment would be a better measure.

The General Electric business screen

The General Electric (GE) business screen is an alternative matrix to the BCG one, and uses more variables. The GE business screen classifies products or businesses by reference to market attractiveness and business strengths. These two principal factors are then further sub-divided into their contributing elements:

◆ *attractiveness* factors include: size, growth rates, competitive diversity and structure, profitability, technological impacts, social impacts, environmental impacts, legal impacts, and human impacts

◆ *business strength* factors include: size, growth rate, market share, profitability, margins, technology position, strengths and weaknesses, image, environmental impact and management.

A GE business screen is constructed by selecting the factors which contribute to market attractiveness and business strength. These factors will vary between industries and between companies operating in the same industry. Once the selection of relevant factors has been made, each of these should be assigned a numerical rating. Each product or business can then be placed in position on the matrix. A completed GE matrix is shown in Fig. 7.6. As can be seen from Fig. 7.6, products or businesses are represented by circles containing the company's market share as a segment of total market size.

Figure 7.7 illustrates the various strategies suggested by the GE matrix. The GE business screen has been criticised because the selection and ranking of market attractiveness and business strengths factors is a subjective process.

 ## Products and brands

According to IBM, the company 'doesn't sell products. It sells solutions to customers' problems'. This reminds us of the different ways that products are perceived by companies and customers. All too often companies look at products in terms of their physical characteristics or the manufacturing process. Customers, on the other hand, look at products in terms of their ability to satisfy needs. P Doyle has this definition of a product:

Product: anything which meets the needs of customers.

T Levitt has argued that products have four levels, as shown in Fig. 7.8. At each of the succeeding levels, further value is added to the product.

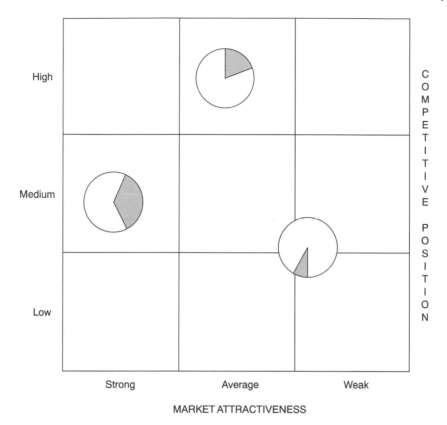

Fig. 7.6 GE business screen

1 *Generic product* This is the basic product type. Sugar is an example of a generic product, as is a telephone.

2 *Expected product* This is the generic product in a form that the customer expects. In the case of sugar, this might be white, refined sugar. In the case of a telephone, the expected product will contain a number of additional features that have become the norm: push-buttons instead of a dial, and a small memory for holding the most frequently-called numbers.

3 *Augmented product* This is the expected product plus additional features or benefits. These are added by companies in an effort to attract customers to their product. Typical areas of product augmentation include design features, product guarantees, delivery, installation and after-sales service, credit facilities and image. The additional features offered by the augmented product are rapidly copied by competitors, and the augmented product thus becomes, in time, the expected product.

4 *Potential product* This consists of further additions to the product to make it more attractive still to customers.

	Strong	Average	Weak
High	Invest/grow	Invest/grow	Strategy uncertain
Medium	Invest/grow	Strategy uncertain	Harvest/divest
Low	Strategy uncertain	Harvest/divest	Harvest/divest

COMPETITIVE POSITION

MARKET ATTRACTIVENESS

Fig. 7.7 Strategies suggested by GE matrix

HIGHER BREADUCATION

For a taste of the real revolution sweeping through Washington, the place to go is not Capitol Hill but the Brick Oven. On the counter of this newly-opened bakery are samples of several exotic-looking loaves: semolina with caraway and sunflower seeds, six-cereal bread, traditional sourdough, 'holiday challah'. 'Four years ago, this area didn't have anything like this,' says the owner, Alan Hakimi.

The squidgy white loaf dominated America for about as long as the Democrats controlled the House of Representatives. Then came the great upheaval of the 1990s. First cappuccino frothed from coast to coast: now trendy bread is on the rise. The number of bread shops 'is just exploding', according to Bill Donahue, who runs a trade publication called 'Modern Baking'.

In many ways, these loaves fit the times. They have little fat or cholesterol. They are an affordable luxury. The smell and warmth of a bakery, especially when the artisan-bakers and their ovens are in view, reach deep into people's associations with homely, old-fashioned values. And the sense of tradition combines with American inventiveness to cater for all modern tastes.

The Economist, 7 October 1995

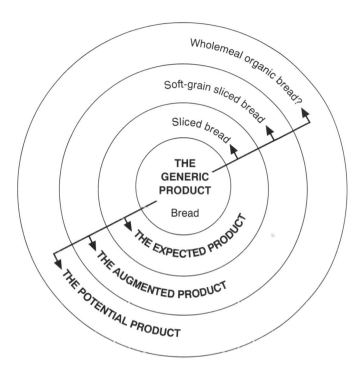

Fig. 7.8 Four levels of product type

Product branding occurs when a product receives an identification that makes it immediately recognisable to customers. Product identification can be given by a name, a company logo or symbol, or through the use of distinctive packaging. The product's name will usually be accompanied by a registered trademark to prevent others from using it. A product which has been identified in one of these ways is known as a brand.

Sometimes a brand name becomes so closely associated with its product that consumers use the brand name when they refer to the product. Hoover and Filofax are both company names that have become synonymous with particular products.

To be successful, a brand must have a sustainable differential advantage over rival products. This means that customers must prefer the brand to rival products, perhaps because the brand has an outstanding reputation for quality or performance. It also means that it must be difficult for other companies to compete against the brand.

Customers purchase brand products for two principal reasons. First, brand products are known by customers, and the selection of a brand product simplifies the purchase process. This is particularly the case where low-cost frequent purchases are concerned. Second, customers are likely to have a positive image of brand products, and so they prefer them.

Brand products achieve high market share because customers prefer them and are loyal to them. This makes them very profitable for companies. The PIMS study in America revealed that products with a market share of 40 per cent have a return on investment three times greater than products with a market share of 10 per cent.

Brand success cannot be achieved through advertising alone, although some brands, like Coca-Cola, are heavily advertised. Brand leaders tend to offer high quality, superior service, and they tend to enter a market early or, at least, become established in the minds of customers ahead of competitors.

Identifying competitors

To identify competitors a company needs to consider the different kinds of competition which exist. These are:

1 *Direct competition* This occurs where companies are offering similar products to the same people. Producers of instant coffee are direct competitors, because customers can choose between several, very similar, products.

2 *Close competition* This occurs where companies are offering the same category of products to customers. Scotch whisky producers are therefore in close competition with French wine producers.

3 *Indirect competition* This occurs where companies are competing for a share of customer income. In August, for example, some families will decide whether to buy a foreign holiday or spend the same money on a deposit for a new car. In such a case, motor manufacturers and holiday companies are in indirect competition with each other. Identifying indirect competitors is extremely difficult.

Competitor objectives and strategies

Having identified its competitors, a company next needs to understand what its competitors' objectives are and the strategies they will use to achieve them.

Evaluations of competitor objectives will take into account factors such as financial resources, manufacturing capacity, known skills areas, and past performance. Marketing intelligence data will come from a variety of different sources and is a subject we will discuss in Chapter 8.

As well as understanding the fundamental objectives of competitors, it is important to know how competition within the market is conducted. This is where knowledge of competitors' strategies is significant. In some markets competition may be principally price-based; in others it may be quality-based. Once the strategies of competitors have been identified, a company is in a position to calculate its own offensive and defensive strategies.

 ## Competitor strengths and weaknesses

We saw in Chapter 3 how a SWOT analysis can be used to match internal company strengths with external opportunities. Analysis of the relative strengths and weaknesses of the company and its competitors can also be carried out by means of a SWOT analysis. Once again it is important that the analysis concentrates on key factors for success.

 ## Predicting competitor behaviour

The fundamental purpose of competitor analysis is to enable a company to predict how its competitors will behave in the future. Detailed competitor intelligence-gathering will assist the prediction process, as will a knowledge of competitor behaviour in the past.

 ## Industry structure and profitability

According to M E Porter's model of competition, which we first mentioned in Chapter 2, company profitability depends on the structure of the industry of which the company is a part. You will remember that Porter identifies five competitive forces: new entrants, suppliers, buyers, substitute products and industry competitors.

Suppliers and customers participate in the value chain connecting raw materials to consumption. Suppliers can affect industrial profitability by manipulating either the prices they charge for their products, or the quality of their products. Where there is a monopoly supplier, as in the case of regional electricity companies, the bargaining strength of suppliers is greatest. Where there are many suppliers, the bargaining strength of suppliers is lowest.

Industrial profitability is also affected by the opportunity that suppliers or customers have to go outside the value chain. This happens in vertical integration when a manufacturer integrates backwards by establishing an independent supply-source, or forwards by establishing an independent distribution system.

Industrial profitability is further affected by the presence of substitute products and new entrants to the industry. Price levels are limited when customers can purchase substitute products, or when new companies enter an industry.

M E Porter recognises three fundamental ways in which an individual company can compete successfully in its industry:

1 *Cost leadership strategy* A company following this strategy seeks to ensure profitability by being a low-cost producer. Low-cost producers can use their advantage to offer competitive prices to their customers, or to invest in product research and development or other investments designed to secure their position in the industry. Low-cost leadership can be achieved by establishing large manufacturing plants, to take advantage of economies of scale. The development of global brands also contributes to successful cost leadership.

2 *Differentiation strategy* A company following this strategy seeks to ensure profitability by offering customers products which are either unique, or which are of a much higher quality than competitors' products. The differentiation strategy calls for the development of a strong brand image to which customers remain loyal.

3 *Focus strategy* A small company which is unable to achieve the economies of scale necessary to become a cost leader, or the kind of product excellence associated with the differentiation strategy, may choose to focus on serving a small customer segment. A company following this strategy must understand the needs of its customers and anticipate how these will change over time.

 ## The experience curve effect

In 1925 the commander of the Wright Patterson airforce in the USA noticed that the time required for building an aeroplane decreased once a certain experience of aeroplane building had been acquired. This phenomenon has since become known as the *experience curve effect*, or the learning curve. The Boston Consulting Group discovered in the 1960s that the experience curve effect could be applied to many aspects of business activity, and not simply production. The experience curve effect is significant for businesses because it indicates that costs can be reduced as a result of increased familiarity with operations.

 # Profit impact of marketing strategies (PIMS)

During the 1960s the Strategic Planning Institute in the USA began to collect and analyse data from a large number of companies, and to give advice based on their studies about the relationship between specific business strategies and net cash flow and profitability.

The Profit Impact of Marketing Strategies (PIMS) research is available to subscribing companies in a number of reports covering the following areas:

◆ The *Par Report* describes normal returns on investment for different business types

◆ The *Strategy Analysis Report* describes the expected results of following different general strategies

◆ The *Optimum Strategy Report* describes what are considered to be the best strategic moves for a specific business

◆ The Report on '*Look Alikes*' gives information on successful strategies employed by similar businesses.

Critics of the PIMS approach argue that the research should not really be used to predict success because it is descriptive in nature, rather than being causal.

 # Marketing as warfare

Defensive and offensive strategies

P Kotler and other writers have explored the analogies between military strategies and competitive strategies for businesses. Four basic marketing strategies have been identified from the military analogy: Defence, Challenge, Follow and Niche.

Defence

The first of the defence strategies is known as the *fortress strategy*. A company choosing this strategy seeks to defend itself against competitors by constructing a 'fortress' of strong products. This is a stationary policy, and

STAR WARS

There is a new space race under way, one as risky as the US government's £25 billion program that put a man on the moon more than two decades ago. This time, though, the risk is being borne by industry. The mission: to profit by transmitting to any spot on earth.

Customers will be dazzled by the services that will be available in the next few years, from roam-anywhere global telephones and detailed photos from space, to futuristic two-way video and data transmissions that will speed everything from meetings to medical treatment. Already, satellite-to-home television, showing live news and sports events from thousands of kilometres away, is enjoying growing success.

But for the pack of mostly American aerospace and communications companies preparing to launch their fortunes, there isn't any assurance of an easy ride. In the market for satellite video and computer conferencing alone, more than a dozen entrants – including General Motor Corp's Hughes Electronics Corp unit, AT&T Corp and General Electric Co – have unveiled a combined $23 billion or more in satellite constellations they plan to launch in the next six years. The field of players is getting crowded so fast that investors are having second thoughts. In recent weeks, separate mobile phone ventures led by Loral Corp and Motorola Inc have had to withdraw a total of $700 million in debt offerings after wary investors demanded too-high returns and guarantees.

'There is a wonderful opportunity with satellites,' says Arno Penzias, chief scientist at AT&T's Bell labs and winner of a Nobel prize for space research in 1978. But in the dash to commercialise space, he sees prides of lions all speeding towards 'a big, fat zebra'. Dr Penzias worries 'there's not going to be much meat there for any one of them'.

Lured by projections of a $160 billion market over the next decade, US companies, large and small, along with a smattering of partners and feisty rivals in Europe and Asia, have begun investing billions of dollars in new generations of satellites and ground receiving systems, as well as in advanced rockets to put the complex birds into orbit.

Many of the proposed satellite and launch systems are untried. Some will use untested orbits. Others will have to link dozens of speeding satellites and ground stations into a seamless network to provide unified service, billing and marketing around the globe.

Another unknown is the true size of each market. Nearly every new player is trying to win the front-end business of producing satellites and rockets and providing launch services. That market alone is valued at a total of $31 billion or more through 2005, according to estimates by Euroconsult in Paris and US industry. But to strike the motherlode, each entrant must also try to secure a share of the $130 billion they expect to flow from delivering all those voices and pictures to consumers and commercial buyers over that period.

The Wall Street Journal Europe, 11 October 1995

is invariably doomed to failure in the long-term, as the company fails to adapt its products to changes in the environment. Over time, individual products fall victim to competitor action or become obsolete, and the company finds itself defending a shrinking fortress of products and markets.

The British motor-cycle industry failed to respond to the Japanese threat to its market by adapting its products and prices, and was eventually driven out of existence.

A second defence strategy is *mobile defence*. Here the company defends itself from competitors through innovation. A company following this strategy identifies the customer needs which its products serve, and becomes involved in all the technologies associated with that need satisfaction. This strategy requires a company to define its business objectives in terms of generic needs. We saw previously that T Levitt argued that the American film industry failed to defend itself from the threats posed by the advent of television because film-makers defined their business in terms of their products, rather than in terms of generic needs. For many years Penguin seemed to have an unassailable position as the dominant producer of low-priced paperback literary classics. When Wordsworth Classics began to appear, offering a range of titles at 99 pence, Penguin was forced to change its approach to the market.

A *pre-emptive defence strategy* consists of attacking a competitor just before it launches an attack of its own. Here the company defends itself by limiting market opportunities to its competitors. It does this either by continually updating and extending its product range to make competitor entry conditions more difficult, or by letting competitors know that attempts to enter its markets will be fended off. Microsoft's linking of its 'Windows '95' software package with access to the internet is an example of this kind of strategy.

A *flank position defence* consists of building up secondary markets around the company's core business interests. This prevents competitors from establishing themselves in a secondary market as a first step towards launching an attack in a core business area. This is a popular strategy with media owners, who frequently protect their interests in one key area by diversifying into related areas. Rupert Murdoch, for example, controls a media network comprising newspapers, magazines and television channels.

A *counter-offensive defence* consists of responding to a competitor attack directly, or through a flanking or pincer movement. This was a strategy adopted by British Airways in its struggle against Richard Branson's Virgin airline.

A *contraction defence* is sometimes adopted by a weak market leader. It consists of abandoning markets or products which come under competitor attack. The company shrinks back to concentrate on markets or products in which it remains relatively unopposed.

Challenge

The market challenger is a company which wants to increase its market share by following an aggressive marketing strategy. A market challenger can attack a market leader, the strategy which carries the highest degree of risk. Successful attacks on market leaders have occurred where the challenger has made a more effective use of new technology. Attacks can also be launched on companies of equal size to the challenger or on smaller companies.

A *frontal attack* is a direct assault on a competitor, and takes the form of matching a rival's products, prices and advertising. In some frontal attacks the challenger attempts to match products and advertising, but offers a lower price in the hope of gaining market share. This can lead to the outbreak of a price war between competitors, a recurring feature in the British newspaper industry. Frontal attacks carry a very high degree of risk for challengers, and most companies prefer to follow an indirect strategy of attack.

A *flanking attack* consists of an indirect attack on a competitor's area of weakness. Flanking attacks are usually concentrated on geographical areas of weakness or market segment areas of weakness. During the 1980s Amstrad successfully mounted a series of flanking attacks on IBM, by offering IBM-compatible computers at much-reduced prices.

Encirclement consists of mounting a generalised attack on a competitor. The purpose of this kind of generalised assault is to reduce the competitor's ability to defend itself. This means that weaknesses appear in the competitor's line of defence which can be breached in the future. Product encirclement occurs when a challenger launches a vast product range which overcomes competitors. Encirclement also occurs when a challenger increases the number of market segments it serves, or the number of distribution outlets it uses. Encirclement strategies are expensive to carry out, and are therefore only appropriate for companies with resources superior to those of their competitors. To be successful, encirclement strategies also depend on having access to distribution channels and product development capacity. Japanese companies came to dominate the hi-fi and audio equipment market by offering a huge range of products, which European and American producers could not match.

A *bypass attack* consists of a challenger establishing itself in areas where there is no competition. This is done by developing new products which satisfy needs not served by the competition. For a challenger to mount a successful bypass attack it is necessary to be already established in a market from which the bypass assault can be launched.

Guerilla attacks consist of mounting much smaller-scale assaults on competitors than any of the other offensive strategies already discussed. Guerilla attacks can be market-focused, concentrating on promotions or price reduction campaigns. They can also be non-market focused, concentrating on publicity campaigns which attack competitors. Guerilla attacks can be effective strategies for smaller challengers who wish to make inroads into markets without seriously threatening the positions of existing leaders.

Follow

Companies which do not have the resources, market position or technological expertise to threaten market leaders are known as market followers. Opportunities for market followers occur in industries where price is an important factor in determining buyer behaviour, and where smaller companies can offer better customer services than the dominant market leaders. Successful strategies for market followers consist of precise market segmentation, so that the follower competes only in market segments where it has relative strength; an emphasis on profitability rather than on sales growth and market share; and a concentration on a small, quality range of products rather than product diversification.

Niche

Many small companies avoid competing with market leaders by focusing on highly-specialised market segments. These are called *niche markets* and can be a source of profitability for smaller companies which concentrate on the satisfaction of their customers' needs. Successful strategies for companies serving niche markets consist of locating a number of markets, keeping track of changing customer needs and requirements and emphasising product quality.

Self-assessment test questions

These questions have been designed to test your recall of the main points in this chapter. The answers can be found on p. 220.

Complete the following sentences:

  1 An estimation of market size is . . .

2 Market growth is an estimation of . . .

3 The BCG matrix concentrates on two variables. These are . . .

4 The GE business screen classifies products or businesses by reference to . . .

5 The four product levels identified by T Levitt are . . .

6 The three strategies for success identified by M E Porter are . . .

7 A pre-emptive defence strategy consists of . . .

8 A market challenger is a company which . . .

9 The purpose of encirclement is to . . .

10 Direct competition occurs where . . .

State whether each of the following statements is TRUE or FALSE:

11 P Kotler has argued that there are three levels of product life-cycle.

12 In the Boston Consulting Group's matrix, 'dogs' are products in decline.

13 The General Electric business screen uses less variables than the BCG matrix.

14 T Levitt has argued that products have three levels.

15 M E Porter recognises four fundamental success strategies.

Write short notes on the following:

16 (a) market size

(b) market share

(c) market growth

17 the Boston Consulting Group's matrix

18 the General Electric business screen

19 direct, close and indirect competition

20 offensive and defensive marketing strategies.

Research activity

In this chapter we have seen that the concept of the product life-cycle is widely used by marketers, although the length of the cycle for any given product is not provided by the concept itself. How might you estimate the probable length of the product life-cycle for the following products:

◆ a 'bestseller' by Jeffrey Archer

◆ a range of toys launched to coincide with the issue of a children's film

◆ a new chocolate bar

◆ a family car?

Types of data

8

After reading this chapter you should be able to:

◆ Distinguish between primary and secondary data

◆ Outline some of the problems associated with using secondary data for marketing

◆ Distinguish between qualitative and quantitative research methods

◆ List the stages in the marketing research process.

As well as generating an enormous amount of information as part of the process of satisfying customer needs, businesses require a lot of additional information for effective decision-making. In this chapter and the next we will consider the information needs of companies, and how these can be met both from sources within the company and from external sources.

The range of data generated and required by a company will obviously depend on the kind of industry the company is involved in, the size of the company, and the complexity of decisions facing it. All companies, however, are likely to require information to assist with decision-making of the following kinds:

◆ *Market decisions* cover such matters as total market size, market segments of particular interest to a company, and the degree of risk associated with market entry.

◆ *Strategic marketing decisions* cover such matters as mode of entry to a market, the competitive position to take, and timing decisions.

◆ *Operational marketing decisions* cover such matters as which elements of the marketing mix to stress when offering products for sale, and the execution of periodic performance reviews.

In order to obtain the information it needs, a company will usually have to convert data from other sources into usable information. Such data comes from three principal sources, as Fig. 8.1 illustrates.

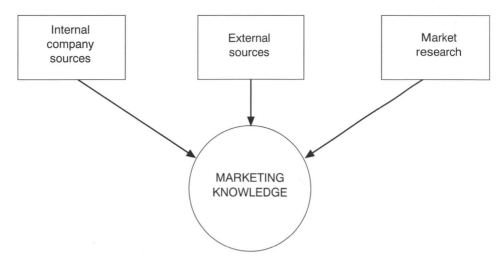

Fig. 8.1 Principal sources of data

 ## Sources of internal secondary data

Secondary data is data that was originally collected for another purpose, but which can be adapted for use by a marketing department. Such data may originate in other departments or in previous research carried out by the marketing department itself. The chief problem with information compiled by other departments is that it tends to be presented in accounting terms, and this is not always the most useful form for marketing analysis. A good marketing information system will be able to render accounting data in more useful forms.

 ## Customer information

Data from the sales department is usually structured to provide the following information:

◆ customer name and address

◆ date of sale

◆ product and quantity ordered

◆ price and discount offered and conditions of sale.

A marketing information system can take such data and use it to obtain the following marketing information:

◆ *customer name and address*: identification and geodemographic customer profiles

◆ *date of sale*: seasonal variations in sales levels can be followed

◆ *product and quantity ordered*: customer needs analysis, and division of customers into heavy or light product users

◆ *price and discount offered and conditions of sale*: customer price sensitivity, service requirements and after-sales warranties.

Further sales department data of relevance will include the total sales records. These can be broken down to give sales information about the following:

◆ *Product types or groups* When a company manufactures a range of products it is important to be able to compare the sales levels for different products or product types.

◆ *Regions* Regional sales levels can vary considerably, and it is important to monitor these.

◆ *Market segments* A company should always keep track of the market segments it is serving, so as to be aware of changes in customer needs.

◆ *Distribution channels* Some distribution channels may be more successful than others, and channel strategies may have to be changed.

Product information

Product information comes mainly from the production department, although useful data can also come from other company sources. Product information of relevance to a marketing information system includes the following:

◆ product performance and technical specifications

◆ product materials, design and style

◆ product size and colour.

Other useful sources of company data include salaries and wages records, and other departmental plans for the future.

Sources of external secondary data

External secondary data is information that was originally gathered by an outside agency for its own purpose, but is later used by a company. There follow examples of this kind of data.

Government sources of data

◆ *Census of Population* Every ten years the government carries out a full survey of the population, from which it prepares information about population numbers, age, sex, marital status, socioeconomic class, country of birth and employment.

◆ *The Annual Abstract of Statistics* and its monthly version, *The Monthly Digest of Statistics*, contain information on the following topics: population, education, labour, energy, building and construction, agriculture and fisheries, transport, communications, the balance of payments, wages and prices, expenditure and wealth, and prices.

◆ *Business Monitors* provide statistical information on production, imports and exports for a range of industries.

◆ *The Digest of UK Energy Statistics* is an annual publication.

◆ *The Census of Production* is an annual publication concerned with manufacturing, mining, electricity, gas and water industries. It provides data on employment levels, wages and salaries, stocks, capital expenditure, materials purchases, sales and work carried out.

◆ *The Employment Gazette* is a monthly publication which gives details of employment levels in different industries, and data on wage-rate changes and hours of work.

◆ *Economic Trends* is a monthly publication which provides data on the value of imports and exports, the volume of retail sales, retail prices, gross domestic product, disposable income, saving and borrowing, consumer expenditure and investment.

◆ *Social Trends* is an annual publication which gives data on population, employment, social security, leisure, health, education, housing, the environment and the law.

◆ *British Business* is a weekly publication which gives data on industrial and commercial trends, both within Britain and overseas.

Although government-generated information is of great value to companies, there are some difficulties about using government statistics for marketing purposes. These statistics are usually designed to help with the formulation of government macro-economic policy, and they may deal in aggregates of data which are too broad to be of much use to the narrower interests of individual companies.

Non-government sources of data

◆ The national and financial press, specialist magazines and journals contain much information of use to businesses.

◆ The research organisation Mintel publishes reports on a wide range of markets. *Mintel Reports* cover such matters as market size, competitors, market share analysis, and significant trends.

◆ The research organisation *Euromonitor* also specialises in the preparation of market reports.

◆ The research organisation *Key Note* differs from Mintel and Euromonitor in that it specialises in the preparation of reports for business-to-business markets.

◆ *The Henley Centre for Forecasting* specialises in the preparation of market reports, as does the Economic Intelligence Unit.

◆ Professional associations, such as the Chartered Institute of Marketing and the British Institute of Management, can be sources of information.

◆ Trade journals and specialist periodicals contain a great deal of information relating to particular industries.

◆ University and public libraries also contain a wealth of information sources for companies.

◆ Retail audits are records of retail sales to consumers, which are prepared and sold by private research companies. This data is of great value to manufacturers and retailers, as it helps them to calculate market shares for different products, and to gauge the effect on sales of sales promotion campaigns and advertising.

◆ Information about companies can be obtained from a number of publications, and is of use because it details company product markets, as well as giving financial information.

Sources of media data

◆ *National Readership Surveys Ltd* provides readership and audience research data for newspapers and magazines.

◆ *The Broadcaster's Audience Research Board* provides audience research data for television stations.

◆ *Radio Joint Audience Research Ltd* provides audience research data for radio stations.

Sources of international data

These sources are of use to companies operating in foreign markets:

◆ *The European Union* publishes a number of studies on matters relating to European trade and industry.

◆ *The General Agreement on Tariffs and Trade* publishes a wealth of information relevant to international business.

 # Computers and data analysis

Quantitative methods have been widely used in production departments for a long time, but it is only comparatively recently that such methods have been used in marketing. The relative delay in the application of quantitative methods in marketing was due to a number of factors. First of these is the complexity of marketing information, and the fact that it is concerned with human behaviour which is difficult to measure. Second is the instability of marketing relationships, which are subject to many changes in market and consumer conditions. Nowadays, however, the use of computers has made the quantitative analysis of data easier and faster, and computer software has been developed for most types of analysis.

What follows is a brief description of the principal quantitative methods used in marketing. It is not necessary at this stage to have greater detail about the methods than is provided here.

1 *Factor analysis* is used for analysing consumer behaviour, market segmentation and product/service attributes. Its purpose is to reduce a large number of variables to a few, discernible factors.

2 *Latent factor analysis* is similar to factor analysis in that its purpose is to identify factors and express the relationships of variables to these. In this kind of analysis, manifest variables are treated as if they are the expression of hidden, underlying traits. Latent analysis has been used in consumer behaviour analysis, segmentation research, and market structure analysis.

3 *Multiple regression analysis* is used to examine the relationship between a dependent variable, such as sales volume, and an independent variable such as price or demand.

4 *Cluster analysis* is used to sort a set of objects into groups or clusters. Consumers, for example, can be sorted into clusters according to age, sex, occupation or income.

5 *Conjoint analysis* is used to assist in the design of products. Consumers are asked to rank the proposed product's attributes, and these rankings are then used to design a product with characteristics that will appeal to the widest number of customers.

6 *Forecasting* Time series forecasting techniques use an analysis of historical data to project trends or patterns into the future. The moving average technique works by calculating the numerical average of a number of consecutive points in a time series. Computer programs exist which take account of factors of distortion in a time series, such as the usual increase in demand for toys at Christmas. A weighted moving average technique works by giving added weight to the more recent points in a time series, on the grounds that these are more relevant to the present. The added weight is calculated by using an arithmetic progression. In more sophisticated time series, the arithmetic progression is replaced by a geometric progression: this technique is known as 'exponential smoothing'. A trend projection consists of forecasting future events by extrapolation from past performance.

7 *Simulation models* have been developed which reduce the need for expensive field research in certain cases. The purpose of simulation models is to reproduce as closely as possible an operational situation. Simulation models have been developed to assist decision-making in the areas of distribution, consumer behaviour, retailing, staffing and advertising.

8 *Artificial intelligence systems* are a further development from simulation. Their purpose is to illustrate and analyse logical thinking in a number of situations. An 'expert' system consists of a program of knowledge or expertise which can be used to generate advice according to sets of rules. Neural networks are programs that aim to reproduce human decision-making. They are designed to be more 'intuitive' than expert systems.

Marketing research

Marketing research has been defined by the American Marketing Association as follows:

> **Marketing research: the systematic gathering, recording, and analysing of data about problems relating to the marketing of goods and services.**

'Marketing research' should not be confused with 'market research', which is a narrower activity contained within the general marketing research function.

The marketing research function has four responsibilities. First is the processing of internal data from other departments within the company as a means of recording company activity. As we have seen, this function may involve transforming routine accounting data into more relevant forms. Second is the reporting of this internal information to interested parties within the company. Third is the maintenance of records and statistics about markets, sales, customers and competitors. Fourth is the evaluation of data. Finally, marketing research has a responsibility to analyse the information maintained so that trends can be anticipated.

There are essentially three ways of classifying marketing research.

One classification is by reference to the way in which information is gathered. This classification distinguishes between 'ad hoc' and 'continuous' marketing research. *Ad hoc research* is research carried out for a specific purpose and is formally presented in a report. *Continuous marketing research* is carried out on a regular basis and is used to assist routine decision-making.

The second classification distinguishes between the types of information collected. Marketing research is separated into *quantitative* and *qualitative* research. Quantitative marketing research expresses information in numerical form and is the commonest method of presenting information to assist the decision-making process. Qualitative marketing research is not expressed in numerical form. Motivational research, which we mentioned in Chapter 3, is a qualitative technique for analysing the psychological drives behind consumer purchase behaviour. This technique allows the researcher to explore a topic in depth with a consumer, and this is the great advantage of all the qualitative methods. Other qualitative techniques include:

◆ *Historical analogy* This works by comparing a new product's growth potential with that of a similar product. Historical analogy rests on the assumption that a new product will behave in similar ways to older products, and this is not always the case.

◆ *Sales force opinion* A company sales force is in close and regular contact with customers, and should therefore have knowledge of customer needs and likely behaviour.

The third classification distinguishes between the fundamental purposes of research. Marketing research is divided into three categories: descriptive, exploratory and causal. *Descriptive* research usually begins with a hypothesis, although not always. In either case, descriptive research is narrower than exploratory research: its main purpose being to establish how something is operating. *Exploratory* marketing research is used to gain initial insights into a situation, rather than conclusions. The purpose of exploratory research is to arrive at a precisely formed hypothesis. *Causal* marketing research is concerned with establishing a causal link between phenomena.

 ## Marketing research process

The marketing research process makes use of what is called the *scientific method*, which has the following stages:

1 *Problem definition and the establishment of research objectives and costs* A research project cannot be undertaken until the marketing problem has been precisely defined. Research objectives should be sufficiently wide to allow relevant data to be considered, but sufficiently narrow to exclude the consideration of irrelevant data. Research costs will be partly dependent on whether the data to be gathered already exists in some form, or whether it will need to be generated during the project.

2 *Development of a research plan* At this stage it will be decided whether the data needed for the research project can be obtained from secondary sources, or whether it will be necessary to gather this information from primary sources. The techniques used to gather primary data include the following: observation, experimentation, sampling, questionnaires and consumer panels. We will discuss the gathering and analysis of primary data in Chapter 9.

3 *Data collection* Desk research can be used to gather internal company data, as well as external secondary data. The gathering of primary data

is known as *field research*. Whatever sources of data are used, it is important that the researcher ensures the data is:

◆ *accurate*: it should be a valid representation of the phenomena being researched; it should come from a reliable source; and it should be sensitive to the individuals being assessed

◆ *current*: it should be up-to-date

◆ *sufficient*: it should be complete

◆ *relevant*: it should be relevant to the phenomena under study.

4 *Data analysis* The purpose of all marketing research is to produce information that assists decision-making. This means that, even where statistical techniques are used to analyse data, the ensuing information should be comprehensible to management.

5 *Report drafting* A marketing research report should indicate the research objectives, explain the methodology used, and give findings in as clear a form as possible.

 ## The scope of marketing research

Marketing research has a very broad scope, as the following examples indicate:

1 *Market research* This includes estimates of market size; analysis of market potential for new and existing products; estimates of market segment sizes; estimates of market share; sales forecasts and the study of market trends. Examples of market research include:

(a) *Market forecasts* These are concerned with assessing the environmental factors which influence the demand for a company's products. A market forecast takes account of macro-environmental PEST factors, secondary and/or primary data on the market concerned, which is used to make a forecast of total demand, and an evaluation of the total market demand for the company's products in the future.

(b) *Sales forecasts* These are estimates of how many products a company is likely to sell in a given period. A sales forecast is therefore more specific than a market forecast, being focused more on company activity than on macro-environmental factors.

2 *Product research* This includes studies of customer satisfaction with products; forecasting of new uses for products; studies of competitive

products; package and design studies; and test marketing. Examples of product research include:

(a) *New product screening* Ideas for new products are subjected to analysis within the company to determine their ability to meet the company's long-term objectives, and whether they have sufficient growth potential to justify the costs of development.

(b) *Test marketing* This consists of putting a small number of units of a new product on the market in a limited number of sales outlets. The purpose of test marketing is to determine how the product is likely to perform if it is fully launched onto the market.

3 *Price research* This includes analysis of demand elasticities, cost analysis and margin analysis.

4 *Promotion research* This includes evaluation of sales promotion effectiveness; analysis of advertising practices; analysis of sales force effectiveness; establishment of sales territories and evaluation of sales methods. An example of promotion research includes:

Advertisement research Several techniques are available for testing the effectiveness of advertisements before they are released and for evaluating advertisement campaigns in terms of communication effect and sales effect.

5 *Distribution research* This includes planning of location and design of distribution centres; analysis of dealer supply requirements and analysis of transport costs.

6 *Economic and business research* This includes economic and business trends and forecasts; social and political trends and competitive intelligence.

 Self-assessment test questions

These questions have been designed to test your recall of the main points in this chapter. The answers can be found on page 221.

Complete the following sentences:

1 The three kinds of information needed by a company are . . .

2 Secondary data is data that . . .

3 The problem with government statistics, from a marketing point of view, is that . . .

4 The first marketing research responsibility is . . .

5 'Ad hoc' marketing research is . . .

6 Continuous marketing research is . . .

7 Quantitative marketing research is . . .

8 Qualitative marketing research is . . .

9 Two examples of product research are . . .

10 Two examples of market research are . . .

State whether each of the following statements is TRUE or FALSE:

11 The purpose of descriptive research is to reveal causal relationships.

12 Secondary data is data originally collected for another purpose.

13 Qualitative research methods are more widely used than quantitative methods.

14 The purpose of factor analysis is to reduce a large number of variables to a few discernible factors.

15 Continuous marketing research is carried out for a specific purpose.

Write short notes on the following:

16 the principal sources of secondary data

17 the scope of marketing research

18 the relationship between market research and marketing research

19 the marketing research process

20 the distinction between exploratory and causal marketing research.

Research activity

A high-street bank is planning a promotional campaign to attract full-time university/college students. The bank has contacted you with a request that you help them to answer the following questions:

1 Has the number of students attending full-time courses increased or decreased in the last three years?

2 What are the most popular courses of study?

3 What percentage of graduates are still unemployed one year after graduating from university?

Use your local library to obtain this information.

9 Survey planning

After reading this chapter you should be able to:

◆ List the principal uses of observational research

◆ Describe the main characteristics of experimentation

◆ List the techniques associated with motivational research

◆ Distinguish between systematic, stratified, multistage, quota and cluster sampling.

 ## Observational research

Observational research is the simplest approach to the gathering of primary data. It is a useful tool for investigating behaviour patterns, although it is not suitable for investigating the causes of behaviour. Observational techniques are used to gauge consumer reactions to product displays in retail outlets, to assist in planning supermarket store layouts, and in traffic-flow studies.

Direct observation entails watching people in a given environment. A hypermarket, for example, may carry out an observational study in its car park to establish whether shoppers arrive singly, in pairs or whether shopping is a family experience. The information gathered in this way could contribute to a feasibility study on providing customers with a playground facility or a family restaurant.

More sophisticated observational techniques are those involving the use of video recording equipment and eye cameras to measure responses to advertisements. Television audience surveys are carried out by means of meters which record channels selected and length of viewing time.

Observational techniques are sometimes used to obtain information without the subjects' knowledge. Looking at what security cameras at a shopping precinct have recorded, for example, can reveal a wealth of information about where and when people shop.

Experimentation

Where observational techniques simply reveal behaviour patterns, the purpose of experimental techniques is to establish a causal relationship between two or more factors. *Experimentation* in marketing takes place both in laboratory conditions and in the normal environment.

Laboratory testing is used in the design of advertisements. It is important to know not only whether a proposed advertisement will be remembered by the audience, but whether the product in the advertisement will be remembered as well. A number of techniques have been developed to test these aspects of advertisements. *Hall tests*, for example, are used to test consumer reactions to new products. Some laboratory tests measure respondents' physiological reactions to advertisements.

Test marketing, which was mentioned in Chapter 8, takes place in the normal environment. The purpose of test marketing is to determine whether a new product is likely to perform well. A small number of product units are placed on sale in areas which are believed to be representative of the market generally, and sales of the product are observed closely.

In controlled test marketing, also known as *minimarket testing*, the focus of research is on the contribution of retail outlet decisions to sales. A product is placed on sale in a number of retail outlets and the researcher is allowed to select how it is displayed and priced.

Both types of test marketing are expensive to carry out, and it is difficult to locate truly representative test market locations. Test marketing also carries the risk that competitors will have an opportunity to plan their response to a new product before it is fully launched on the market.

The principal disadvantage of using experimental techniques is the difficulty of designing an experiment in the normal environment which is truly scientific, because of the number and complexity of variables which govern human behaviour.

 # Motivational research

Motivational research is a qualitative technique used to investigate the hidden motives behind customer behaviour. Motivational research can take the form of in-depth interviews, group discussions, word association tests, and cartoon tests.

Motivational research has been criticised by some people for being insufficiently scientific, and by others for invading consumer privacy. Despite these criticisms, its proponents claim that this technique is a powerful tool for understanding the reasons behind consumers' product preferences and choices.

Survey research

Survey research is the most important way in which primary data is collected by companies. It differs from observational research because of the respondents' participation in the research, and differs from experimentation in that its main aim is to gather descriptive rather than causal data.

Sampling

Some companies with a very small number of customers find that they can contact all of them directly, in which case they are said to be taking a census of their customers. Usually, however, a company cannot contact all of its customers directly, because it would be too costly or impracticable to do so. In these circumstances it is still possible to conduct a survey, but to do so it becomes necessary to obtain a representative sample of customers.

The principle of sampling is that a small number of consumers within a total consumer 'population' can be representative of the consumer population as a whole, if the process of sample selection is random, and if the sample size is large enough. 'Random' in this context means that there is an equal chance for every member of the population to be selected for inclusion in the sample. For a sample to be genuinely random it is necessary to have access to a sampling frame, which is a list of everyone in the given population.

Simple random sampling

There are two ways to select a random sample from a sampling frame. First, sample members can be selected by a lottery method designed to give every member of the population an equal chance of being included in the sample. It would be possible, by this method, to allocate every employee in a company a number. The sample numbers could then be drawn in such a way that every employee had an equal chance of being selected. Second, the researcher can select the sample by reference to random number tables. Random number tables can be generated easily by computer.

Sometimes it is possible to obtain a sampling frame for a given population, but very often this is impossible, too costly or impracticable for companies. Other techniques have been developed for obtaining samples, some of which approximate to being genuinely random, and others of which do not.

Systematic sampling

Systematic sampling is a way of selecting a sample from a known population. This method does not result in a truly random sample, but is good enough for most purposes. If a company wants to take a sample of 50 customers out of 500, its sampling interval would be 500 divided by 50, that is 10. The company could then select a first representative at random, and thereafter select every 10th unit of population.

Stratified sampling

A stratified sample consists of a population which has been divided into different groups. A motor vehicle manufacturer, for example, might sell 5 per cent of its products to government departments, 25 per cent to businesses, and the remaining 70 per cent to individuals. A stratified sample would reflect these strata: 5 per cent of the sample would be government departments, 25 per cent would be businesses, and 70 per cent individuals.

Consumer stratification can be carried out by dividing a consumer population into groups by reference to gender, age, region, or other variables.

Multistage sampling

The purpose of multistage sampling is to reduce the costs of carrying out a survey. This is done by focusing enquiries on a limited number of areas. In a national survey, for example, it would be necessary to visit a number of respondents in different areas to obtain a random sample of the population. This problem is reduced by dividing the country into areas and sampling these areas on a random basis. From this sample another, smaller sample is then obtained. The process can be repeated until a manageable number of people have been selected. Figure 9.1 shows how multistage sampling can be organised.

Cluster sampling

In cluster sampling the population is reduced in the same way as in multistage sampling. The researcher is then instructed to approach every person in the defined area who has certain characteristics. The purpose of cluster sampling is to locate a sample.

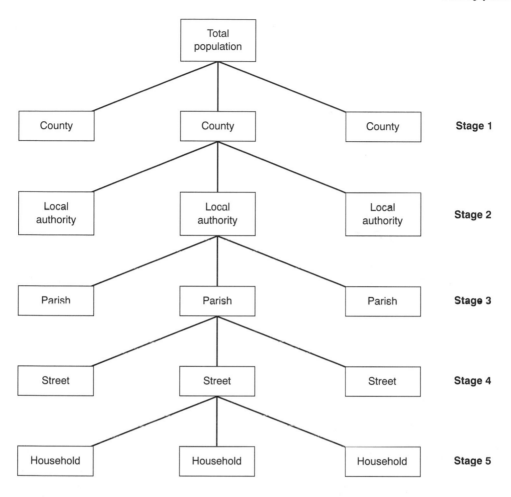

Fig. 9.1 Multistage sampling

Quota sampling

In quota sampling the researcher is instructed to approach a predetermined number, or quota, of people. The researcher selects the survey respondents, but is given instructions on how this is to be done. In a quota of one hundred people, for example, the researcher may be told that 50 respondents must be men and 50 must be women. Each of these two basic groups can be further sub-divided by reference to class, age, or other variables. Quota sampling is not genuinely random because the sample selection is made by the researcher, and so it is not possible to measure sampling error statistically.

Selection of a sample size

In a random sample there is a statistical relationship between the size of the sample selected and the accuracy of the survey results. It is usual to approach the issue of sample size by determining in advance the degree of precision required, and to balance this against the research budget, using the formula:

$$Sample\ size = \frac{Total\ budget}{Variable\ cost\ per\ interview}$$

Postal surveys

Postal surveys are relatively easy to design and administer. Their associated costs are low and their use precludes interviewer bias which might distort the survey results. Despite these advantages, however, there are a number of problems which need to be borne in mind. First, the response rate to unsolicited postal questionnaires is very low, in the range of 2 to 3 per cent. This means there is always a risk that the people who do respond are not typical of the population under examination.

Telephone interviews

Telephone interviewing is a popular way of gathering primary data and has the following advantages: it is relatively inexpensive; many people can be reached who would not complete a postal survey questionnaire; and it is an effective method for obtaining simple information quickly and easily. Against these advantages, however, must be weighed the following disadvantages: telephone interviews have to be kept short and simple, and so there is little opportunity for an in-depth analysis of issues, and it is not possible to use telephone interviews to obtain confidential information.

Personal interviews

Although personal interviewing is the most expensive method of gathering primary data, it has several advantages over the other methods. First, it is possible to use the personal interview to obtain complicated information where this cannot be done through postal surveys or telephone interviewing. Second, the researcher can probe for additional, or sensitive, information. There is always a risk with personal interviews that results will be distorted by interviewer bias.

Group discussions

A group discussion normally involves between 5 and 25 respondents. This technique is used to gauge reactions to new product ideas and promotional and packaging schemes. A group discussion can be recorded on video-tape for later analysis.

Consumer panels

A consumer panel is a semi-permanent group of consumers who agree to record data in a diary. Typical data entries for a specific product will include where and when the product was purchased, the price paid, and the type of retail outlet used. It is difficult to ensure that the composition of a consumer panel is truly representative of the consumer population as a whole and there is sometimes a tendency for panel members to think of themselves as 'experts' because of their involvement in the research. Despite these disadvantages, however, the consumer panel method can reveal a lot of information to companies about consumer buying habits and trends.

Retail audits

A retail audit consists of a panel of retail outlets which record sales information for a research agency. A researcher visits each of the participating outlets on a regular basis and records the following information:

◆ opening stock for the period

◆ deliveries since last audit

◆ present stockholding

◆ customer sales during the period.

This information is then sold on to manufacturers who can use it to assess their performance.

Designing questionnaires

Questionnaires are used to obtain information about a range of topics, such as consumer habits, opinions, knowledge, attitudes, motivations or lifestyle.

Experience has shown that questionnaires work most effectively when their purpose is made clear to respondents, when they have a simple, easy-to-follow structure, and when they are not too lengthy. The questionnaire should begin with simple questions and move on towards more challenging or sensitive ones as the respondents' confidence grows.

Questionnaires are of four basic types:

1 *Structured, non-disguised questionnaire* The purpose of this questionnaire is made clear to respondents, who are asked to complete a prescribed number of questions. The results from this kind of questionnaire are easy to translate into numerical form for analysis.

2 *Unstructured, non-disguised questionnaire* The purpose of this questionnaire is made clear to respondents, who are asked a general list of questions designed to probe the respondents' reactions to the topic. This kind of in-depth interview is used to obtain exploratory information and carries a degree of risk of bias. It is impossible to translate the results of this kind of interview into numerical form.

3 *Structured, disguised interview* The purpose of this interview is not revealed to respondents, who are asked to answer a prescribed number of questions. This kind of interview is difficult to design, but useful because its results can be translated into numerical form.

4 *Unstructured, disguised interview* The purpose of this interview is not revealed to respondents, who are asked a general list of questions designed to probe initial reactions to the topic. This kind of interview is difficult to design and administer, and is used in psychological research. Its results cannot be translated into numerical form.

Questions in interviews are of three main types:

◆ *closed dichotomous questions* are ones in which the respondent's answer is limited to 'Yes', 'No', or 'Don't know'

◆ *closed multiple-choice questions* are ones in which the respondent must select between several possible answers

◆ *open-ended questions* are ones to which respondents are not guided in giving an answer but may say what they like. Open-ended questions are cumbersome to record and difficult to analyse, but they provide a wealth of information.

There are a number of ways in which data provided by respondents can be measured. One of the most popular of these is the *Likert scale*, which works by asking respondents to rate how strongly they agree or disagree with a statement.

A second way in which data provided by respondents can be measured is by use of a *semantic differential scale*. A semantic differential scale indicates both the direction and intensity of a respondent's knowledge or beliefs of a topic.

 ## Measures

The marketing researcher needs to distinguish between several different uses of numbers. In particular, it is important to note the following:

◆ *Ordinal numbers* are used to identify items in a list. For example:

1   Customers
2   Retailers
3   Distributors
4   Manufacturers.

◆ *Nominal numbers* are used to count data that is sorted into categories. Nominal numbers can be used to prepare frequency distributions or bar charts. The following numbers below show how often 20 people go to the cinema every year.

3   Never
2   Once a year
3   Twice a year
3   Three times a year
2   Four times a year
3   Five times a year
4   More than five times a year.

◆ *Ordinal scales* are used to order items from 'most' to 'least', as in the question *'Put the following holidays in order of preference: camping, sailing, fishing, cycling, walking (1= most preferred, 5= least preferred).'* A respondent might arrange the holidays thus:

1   Sailing
2   Cycling
3   Fishing
4   Walking
5   Camping.

It is not possible with an ordinal scale like this to measure the 'distance' between responses. An ordinal scale can be used to calculate medians and correlations on the ranked data.

◆ *Interval numbers* do have a fixed distance between them, although they have an arbitrary starting-point. A thermometer, for example, has an interval scale.

◆ A ruler has a *ratio scale* rather than an interval scale because it begins with zero.

 ## Uses of company databases

In the last two chapters we have discussed the wealth of information which companies make use of, and generate, as part of the overall process of satisfying their customers. We have mentioned that computers are increasingly being used to store customer information and to analyse data from marketing research.

Computers not only make the processing of routine company data easier and more efficient, they also make it possible to record data on a much greater scale than was previously possible. Supermarkets now use electronic point of sale (EPOS) tills, which allow detailed studies of purchases to be carried out. Credit card records provide further information about individual users' buying habits. Additionally, specialist marketing databases are now available to on-line subscribers. Some of the best-known of these are:

◆ FT Profile

◆ Bank of England Databank

◆ Nielsen Retail Index

◆ Reuter Monitor

◆ National Readership Survey.

This data explosion has led some analysts to believe that 'mass marketing' is now giving way to 'micro-marketing', in which companies can use their computer databases to foster relationships with individual customers. As we move into the increasingly interactive use of computers, it is envisaged that communications between customers and companies will be more frequent, and that customers will play a more active role in shaping company activity. Some of the commonest uses of computers in the company-customer relationship include:

◆ customer interaction records, featuring enquiries, sales, service, payments

◆ correspondence, mail shots, invoicing.

As we have already seen, computers can also play an important role in the development of survey questionnaires and in sampling procedures and the analysis of data. Software packages for marketing research are now available which allow small companies to run research which would previously have been prohibitively expensive for them.

A competitive database can be used to co-ordinate information about competitors from external sources, with company-generated information. A relational database can sort information from a number of different sources by topic.

A sales database can be used to evaluate sales levels over time, salesforce performance, and customer profiles. The ACORN system, for example, classifies consumers according to residential category by reference to their postcode (see Fig. 9.2).

(Overleaf) Fig. 9.2 A postal questionnaire which classifies consumers according to the ACORN system

IMPORTANT: To enter in next month's Prize Draw, please complete and return this questionnaire in the next 10 days. Please feel free to ignore any questions you prefer not to answer – completion is not necessary for your guarantee.

A Registering your ownership:
By filling in these details, you will help Micromark to get in touch with you if necessary about your purchase and about new products.

1 Please give your name in the way you should be addressed.

1 ☐ Mr   2 ☐ Mrs   3 ☐ Ms   4 ☐ Miss   5 ☐ Other title

CQB 03

First name   Initial   Surname

Address

Postcode

2 Date of purchase
Day   Month   Year | 9 |

3 What product have you just purchased? (Tick only ONE)

1 ☐ Torch/Lantern
2 ☐ Decorative Lighting
3 ☐ Security Lighting
4 ☐ Fans, (Desk, etc.)
5 ☐ Ceiling Fans
6 ☐ Electric Heater
7 ☐ Bell Chimes
8 ☐ Workwear
9 ☐ Flying Insect Killer
10 ☐ Domestic Appliances

What is the model number (see carton for model no.)

MM

B About your purchase:
Micromark is keen to listen to their customers to learn about their changing needs. Your answers – and those of other customers – will be a great help to them.

4 Did you receive this product as a gift?

1 ☐ Yes   2 ☐ No

5 Where was this product purchased? (Tick only ONE)

1 ☐ Don't know, received as a gift.
2 ☐ Do It All
3 ☐ Great Mills
4 ☐ Texas
5 ☐ Homebase
6 ☐ Other DIY Superstore
7 ☐ John Lewis
8 ☐ Debenhams
9 ☐ Allders
10 ☐ Owen Owen
11 ☐ Other Dept. store
12 ☐ Woolworths
13 ☐ Fads/Homestyle

14 ☐ Argos
15 ☐ Boots
16 ☐ Other Chemists
17 ☐ Asda
18 ☐ Rumbelows/Atlantis
19 ☐ Currys
20 ☐ Comet
21 ☐ Electricity Board Showroom
22 ☐ Independent Electrical Shop
23 ☐ Specialist Lighting Shop
24 ☐ Independent Hardware Shop
25 ☐ Garden Centre
26 ☐ Mail Order
27 ☐ Other

6a Is this product for use . . .

1 ☐ . . . at home   OR   2 ☐ . . . in commercial premises?

6b If for use at home, in which room do you intend mainly to use it? (Tick only ONE)

1 ☐ Kitchen
2 ☐ Lounge
3 ☐ Bathroom
4 ☐ Bedroom
5 ☐ Dining Room
6 ☐ Hall
7 ☐ Porch
8 ☐ Exterior of house
9 ☐ Garden
10 ☐ Other

7 Which TWO factors most influenced the choice of this product? (Tick no more than TWO)

1 ☐ Did not choose/received as a gift
2 ☐ Micromark reputation
3 ☐ Price/value for money
4 ☐ Colour
5 ☐ Salespersons recommendation
6 ☐ Friend/relatives recommendation
7 ☐ Saw a demonstration
8 ☐ Other

8 Where did you FIRST learn of this Micromark product (Tick only ONE)

1 ☐ TV advertisement
2 ☐ Magazine advertisement
3 ☐ Newspaper advertisement
4 ☐ Previous experience of Micromark
5 ☐ In-store display
6 ☐ Other

C About you:
Micromark would also like to know more about you as a person - it helps when designing new products and planning advertising. Knowing more about you also helps Consumerlink and other respected organisations to ensure that, if you choose to receive information by post, it will interest you.

9 Is the person whose name appears above:

1 ☐ Male?   or   2 ☐ Female?

10 Date of birth of person whose name appears above:
Month   Year | 9 |

11 Marital status:

1 ☐ Married
2 ☐ Widowed
3 ☐ Divorced/Separated
4 ☐ Single/never married

12 Occupation:

	You	Spouse
Professional/senior management	1 ☐	1 ☐
Manager in business	2 ☐	2 ☐
Administrator/clerical	3 ☐	3 ☐
Manual	4 ☐	4 ☐
Housewife	5 ☐	5 ☐
Student	6 ☐	6 ☐
Retired	7 ☐	7 ☐
Other	8 ☐	8 ☐
Self-employed/business owner	9 ☐	9 ☐

13 Please indicate the ages of ALL children living at home:

☐ None
☐ Under 1
☐ 1 yr
☐ 2 yrs
☐ 3 yrs
☐ 4 yrs
☐ 5 yrs
☐ 6 yrs
☐ 7 yrs
☐ 8 yrs
☐ 9 yrs
☐ 10 yrs
☐ 11 yrs
☐ 12 yrs
☐ 13 yrs
☐ 14 yrs
☐ 15yrs
☐ 16 yrs
☐ 17 yrs
☐ 18 yrs
☐ 19 & over

14 Which group best describes your annual family income?

1 ☐ Under £5,000 (Under £96 per week)
2 ☐ £5,000-£7,499 (£96-£144 p.w.)
3 ☐ £7,500-£9,999 (£145-£192 p.w.)
4 ☐ £10,000-£12,499
5 ☐ £12,500-£14,999
6 ☐ £15,000-£17,499
7 ☐ £17,500-£19,999
8 ☐ £20,000-£22,499
9 ☐ £22,500-£24,999
10 ☐ £25,000-£29,999
11 ☐ £30,000-£34,999
12 ☐ £35,000 & above

15 Which of the following do you use regularly?

1 ☐ American Express, Diners Club
2 ☐ Barclaycard, other Visa card, Access, other Master Card
3 ☐ Department store, shop, petrol, hotel credit card(s)
4 ☐ Bank cheque guarantee card
5 ☐ Airline club/frequent flyer programme
6 ☐ None of the above

16 Thinking about your own home, do you:

1 ☐ Own, or are buying, a house, flat or maisonette?
2 ☐ Rent a private house, flat or maisonette?
3 ☐ Rent a council house, flat or maisonette?
4 ☐ Live with parents/guardians?

17 How long have you been at your present address?

1 I only moved here [____] months ago, OR

2 I've lived here for [____] years

NOW PLEASE TURN OVER

130

micromark
QUALITY THAT'S GUARANTEED

This product is guaranteed for twelve months from date of purchase

Thank you for choosing this quality product from Micromark. We hope that it will give you many years of excellent service. Please fill in this questionnaire. The information you give will be held and processed by Consumerlink.

What is the questionnaire for?
It has four purposes

1 **Product Registration.** By filling in part A overleaf you are registering your ownership of the product. Then it's easy for Micromark to contact you if necessary about your purchase and about new products.

2 **Collecting Marketing Information.** By filling in parts B and C it is also your chance to talk to Micromark about you and your needs - this will not affect your guarantee or legal rights.

3 **Keeping You Informed.** If you have no obligations to post you might find interesting according to your answers in parts A and C. You can choose not to share in this opportunity by ticking the box at the end of this questionnaire.

4 **You Could Win a Cheque for £25!** To show our appreciation for your help in returning this questionnaire, a FREE PRIZE DRAW is held on the Friday of each month from all questionnaires received since the previous draw. The licky winners will receive a £25 cheque from Micromark through the post.

Thank you for your help and good luck in the draw!

Consumerlink

Second fold

POST NOW TO BE ENTERED IN THE NEXT FREE DRAW!

(Please do not send products or correspondence to this address)

PLACE STAMP HERE

**MICROMARK
C/O CONSUMERLINK
P.O. BOX 362
LONDON SW11 3UD**

CQB 03

Please seal here with tape.

First fold

18 To help us understand your leisure interests, please indicate the activities and interests which you or your spouse enjoy on a REGULAR basis:

1 Bicycle touring/racing	13 Crossword puzzles	25 Slimming
2 Golf	14 Eating out	26 Fashion clothing
3 Jogging/physical fitness	15 Gardening	27 Model making
4 Snow skiing	16 Grandchildren	28 Photography
5 Squash	17 Household pets	29 Science fiction
6 Tennis	18 Motoring	30 Sewing/needlework/knitting
7 Bowls	19 Motorcycles	31 Stereo, records and tapes
8 Hiking/walking	20 Car maintenance	32 Book reading
9 Fishing	21 Do-it-yourself	33 Current affairs
10 Hunting/shooting	22 Doing the pools	34 Fine art/antiques
11 Motor/power boating	23 Going to the pub	35 Gourmet cooking/fine foods
12 Sailing	24 Health foods	36 Wines

37 Theatre, cultural/arts events	49 Stocks and shares
38 Religious activities	50 Unit trusts/investment programmes
39 Caravanning/caravan camping	51 Cards, board games
40 Package holidays	52 Further education
41 Foreign travel	53 Home computer games
42 Charities/voluntary work	54 Personal computing
43 National Trust	55 Science/new technology
44 Wildlife/environmental concerns	56 Watching video films
45 Coin/stamp collecting	57 Watching sports on TV
46 Collectibles/collections	58 Cigarette smoking
47 Going to bingo	59 Pipe/cigar smoking
48 Shopping by catalogue	

19 From the list above, please indicate the numbers representing the three favourite activities for:

You:

Your Spouse:

20 Do you have a car?

1 Yes 2 No

Is it:
3 Yours?
or 4 A company car?

Make of car
(e.g. Austin Rover, Vauxhall, Ford)

Model of car
(e.g. Metro, Cavalier, Escort)

Year 1 9 or letter of registration

Thank you for completing this questionnaire. We promise to take great care of the information you have provided. As mentioned before, Consumerlink offers you the chance to receive information from other respected organisations, about products and services that relate to your answers in Part C but if you would prefer NOT to receive these details please tick here ☐.

If you have any comments or questions about the services of Micromark or Consumerlink please write to:

Micromark,
550 White Hart Lane,
London,
N17 7RQ

Consumerlink Ltd.
Port House,
Square Rigger Row,
London SW11 3TY

170892

Self-assessment test questions

These questions have been designed to test your recall of the main points in this chapter. The answers can be found on p. 221.

Complete the following sentences:

 1 Observational techniques reveal behaviour patterns, whereas experimentation . . .

 2 The principal disadvantage of using experimentation techniques is the difficulty of . . .

 3 The principle of sampling is that a small number of consumers . . .

 4 A sampling frame is . . .

 5 Systematic sampling is a way of selecting a sample from a . . .

 6 In quota sampling the researcher is instructed to . . .

 7 Closed dichotomous questions are ones in which . . .

 8 Closed multiple-choice questions are ones in which . . .

 9 The Likert scale works by asking respondents to . . .

10 A semantic differential scale indicates both the . . .

State whether each of the following statements is TRUE or FALSE:

11 Observational research is designed to probe consumer motivations.

12 Experimentation in marketing takes place both in laboratory conditions and in the normal environment.

13 The main purpose of survey research is to gather causal data.

14 The response rate to postal questionnaires is 20 to 30 per cent.

15 Personal interviewing is the most expensive method of gathering primary data.

Write short notes on the following:

16 observational research

17 experimentation

18 postal surveys and telephone interviews

19 questionnaire design

20 the Likert scale.

Research activity

Your local radio station wants to assess the feasibility of a weekly one-hour programme, provisionally called 'Business and Consumer Focus'. The programme will feature interviews with local business personalities and give a round-up of consumer news.

The station manager has asked you to design a questionnaire which will be enclosed in the weekend copy of the local newspaper. The purpose of the questionnaire is to find out the following information from respondents:

◆ how frequently they listen to the radio station

◆ the time of day they listen to the radio station

◆ what kinds of programmes they like

◆ whether they are in favour of the idea for the new programme, and when they would prefer it to be scheduled, i.e. day of the week and time of day

◆ their ideas about the programme content.

Design the questionnaire.

10 Analytical techniques

After reading this chapter you should be able to:

◆ **Distinguish between the arithmetic mean, the median and the mode**

◆ **Explain the technique of time series analysis**

◆ **Construct a frequency table**

◆ **Explain what is meant by positive and negative correlation**

◆ **Interpret data given in economic indicators.**

We have seen in the last two chapters that marketing professionals need to be familiar with various types of data, some of which is numerical in form. In this chapter we will look at how this kind of data can be presented, and at some mathematical concepts that are useful for the interpretation of numerical data.

 ## Data presentation

As we saw in our discussion of marketing research in Chapter 8, it is important to present research findings in a clear and attractive way so that they can be easily understood. Here we will examine some ways in which numerical data can be presented.

The easiest way of presenting numerical data is by arranging it into a table. Table 10.1 shows how five sales representatives have performed in a year.

Table 10.1   Sales representatives' performance, 1994–95

Sales representative	Sales objective (£)	Sales achieved (£)	Success (%)
Andrew Duffy	2 000 000	1 500 000	75.00
James Thomson	1 500 000	750 000	50.00
Louisa Brown	1 500 000	1 500 000	100.00
Jack Hammond	1 000 000	1 300 000	130.00
Peter Creak	1 000 000	750 000	75.00

A pie chart can be used to give a visual sense of how each part compares to the others within the whole. Figure 10.1 shows the market share by volume of an imaginary industry which is dominated by five companies.

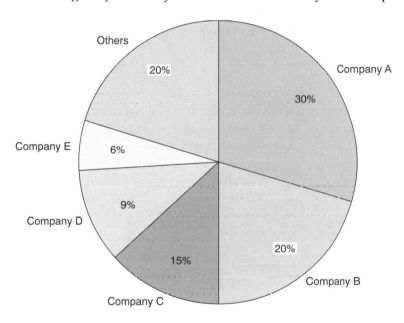

Fig. 10.1 Pie chart to illustrate market share by volume

Bar charts can also be used to give a visual sense of data. Bar charts can be vertical or horizontal, as Figs. 10.2 and 10.3 illustrate.

 Measures of central tendency

The middle values of numerical data can be examined by three measures of central tendency. It is important to understand these measures and how to calculate them.

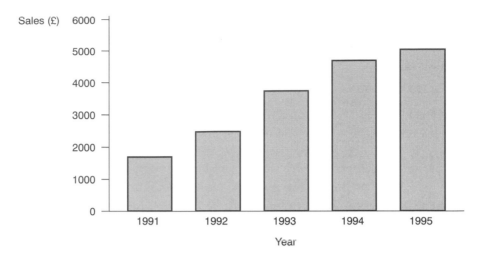

Fig. 10.2 Vertical bar chart to illustrate total yearly sales

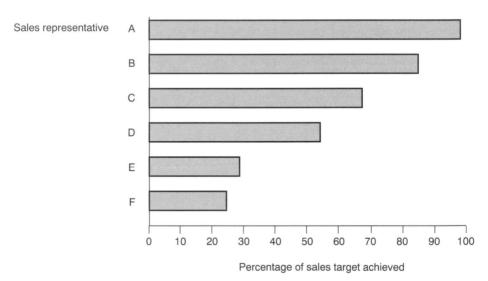

Percentage of sales target achieved

Fig. 10.3 Horizontal bar chart to illustrate sales representatives' achievement of sales targets

1 *The arithmetic mean* This is obtained by adding together the values in a list, and then dividing by the number of items in the list. In the following list five people have been asked how many books they read in a year and their answers have been recorded:

1. 3
2. 5
3. 10

136

4. 20
5. 32

To obtain the arithmetic mean, we add together the total number of books read, which comes to 70. Then we divide 70 by the number of responses, which is 5. Thus 70 divided by 5 produces an arithmetic mean of 14.

The disadvantage of the arithmetic mean is that it can give a distorting impression if some values in a list are very high or very low. This would be the case if the answers to our reading survey were as follows:

1. 3
2. 5
3. 10
4. 20
5. 52

The total number of books read is now 90, and the arithmetic mean is therefore 18. Although it is true to say that respondents in our reading survey read an average of 18 books a year, 60 per cent of respondents read much less than this.

2 *The mode* This is the most frequently-occurring value in a series. In the following list five people have been asked to say how many hours they watch television per day and their answers have been recorded:

1. 1
2. 2
3. 4
4. 4
5. 5

The most commonly-occurring response is 4 hours per day, and the mode is therefore 4. This list of numbers is *unimodal* because there is only one mode. In this second list, however, there are two modes, and the list is therefore *multimodal*:

1. 2
2. 2
3. 3
4. 4
5. 4

3 *The median* This is the figure occurring in the middle of a series arranged in numerical order. In the series 8, 17, 22, the median is 17.

Time series analysis

Time series analysis is a technique for discovering patterns in a company's sales volume over a given time. It relies on relevant historical data such as sales records. The assumption behind time series analysis is that the past pattern of sales can be used to predict future sales. The following figures show the number of televisions sold in a retail outlet for a six-month period:

Month	Sales	Month	Sales
1	30	4	25
2	20	5	35
3	40	6	35

This information can be represented on a graph, as shown in Fig. 10.4. Although the graph shows sales levels rising and falling, it does not indicate whether the tendency of sales is to increase or decrease over time. To discover the underlying trend, we need to use a statistical device called the *moving average*. The moving average reduces the size of peaks and troughs to reveal whether the sales trend is upward or downward. To calculate the moving average, we need the weekly sales for the period under consideration, which are given in Table 10.2.

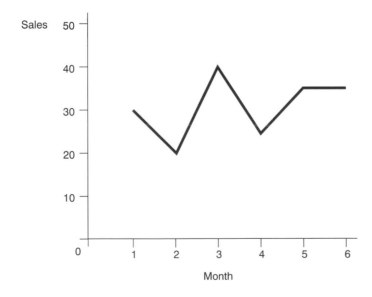

Fig. 10.4 Number of televisions sold over a sixth-month period

Table 10.2   Weekly television sales for six-month period

Month	Week	Sales	Month	Week	Sales
1	1	7	4	13	6
	2	4		14	6
	3	6		15	6
	4	13		16	7
2	5	5	5	17	7
	6	4		18	8
	7	7		19	8
	8	4		20	12
3	9	10	6	21	10
	10	8		22	10
	11	8		23	8
	12	14		24	7

The moving average is calculated by working out the four-week moving totals. The first four-week moving total is 7+4+6+13 = 30. The second four-week moving total is 4+6+13+5 = 28. The third four-week moving total is 6+13+5+4 = 28, and so on. The four-week moving totals can be added to the table, as Table 10.3 now shows.

Table 10.3   Weekly sales for six-month period – moving totals added

Month	Week	Sales	Moving totals	Month	Week	Sales	Moving totals
1	1	7	–	4	13	6	36
	2	4	–		14	6	34
	3	6	–		15	6	32
	4	13	30		16	7	25
2	5	5	28	5	17	7	26
	6	4	28		18	8	28
	7	7	29		19	8	30
	8	4	20		20	12	35
3	9	10	25	6	21	10	38
	10	8	29		22	10	40
	11	8	30		23	8	40
	12	14	40		24	7	35

The four-week moving averages can now be calculated by dividing the four-week moving totals by four. Thus the first four-week moving average is $30/4 = 7.5$, and the second is $28/4 = 7$, and so on. The four-week moving averages can now be added to Table 10.3 to form Table 10.4.

Table 10.4   Weekly sales for six-month period – Moving averages added

Month	Week	Sales	Moving totals	Moving averages
1	1	7	–	–
	2	4	–	–
	3	6	–	–
	4	13	30	7.50
2	5	5	28	7.00
	6	4	28	7.00
	7	7	29	7.25
	8	4	20	5.00
3	9	10	25	6.25
	10	8	29	7.25
	11	8	30	7.50
	12	14	40	10.00
4	13	6	36	9.00
	14	6	34	8.50
	15	6	32	8.00
	16	7	25	6.25
5	17	7	26	6.50
	18	8	28	7.00
	19	8	30	7.50
	20	12	35	8.75
6	21	10	38	9.50
	22	10	40	10.00
	23	8	40	10.00
	24	7	35	8.75

The moving averages can now be added to our original graph (Fig. 10.4) to show the underlying trend of sales during the six-month period. The trend line can be extended into the future to give a forecast of future sales levels.

The weakness of moving averages is that the smoothing process can hide the occurrence of new trends. This effect can be reduced by the process of *exponential smoothing*. Exponential smoothing consists of giving a weighting to the last in the series of moving averages, in order to take account of recent events that might be otherwise obscured.

Frequency distribution

Sometimes a business will accumulate so much numerical data that the calculation of the arithmetic mean becomes a cumbersome operation. Such data can be more easily handled if it is put into a frequency table. The following figures are the number of sales calls made by a representative in the last ten days: 3, 6, 2, 7, 4, 1, 7, 2, 5, 4. The total number of calls is 41 and the arithmetic mean is therefore 41/10 = 4.1.

In the first column of the frequency table (Table 10.5) we can record the different number of calls made in a day. In the second column we can record the frequency with which each number recurs. In the third column we can multiply the number of daily calls by their frequency of occurrence to obtain the total number of calls made.

Table 10.5   Frequency table of a representative's daily calls

Daily calls (x)	Frequency (f)	Calls × Frequency (fx)
1	1	1
2	2	4
3	1	3
4	2	8
5	1	5
6	1	6
7	2	14
Total *f* **10**		Total *fx* **41**

The arithmetic mean can now be obtained by dividing the total number of calls made by the total frequency, which gives 41/10 = 4.1.

 Correlation

Sometimes it is important to know how close the relationship between two or more variables is. The following figures show sales levels of biscuits at different prices:

Sales	Price in pence
100	30
300	28
500	25
600	22
1100	18

This information can be plotted on a scattergram (see Fig. 10.5). A 'line of best fit', known as a *regression line*, can be drawn between the points on the scattergram to show how closely price and demand (sales) are related (see Fig. 10.6). In this case the correlation is high. It is also a negative correlation, because as the value of the independent variable (price) rises, the value of the dependent variable (demand) falls.

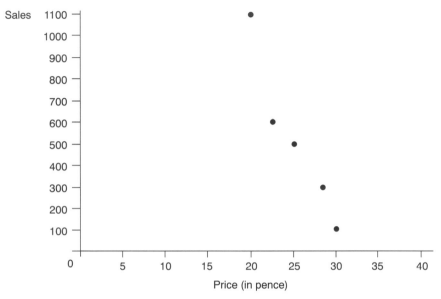

Fig. 10.5 Scattergram of sales of biscuits

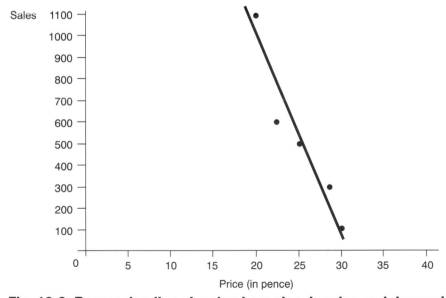

Fig. 10.6 Regression line showing how closely price and demand (sales) are related

In this example, the following figures are concerned with the relationship between the number of foreign holidays taken per year and income:

Number of holidays (per year)	Income level (£)
0	5000
1	8000
1	10 000
2	15 000
2	18 000
3	25 000
4	35 000

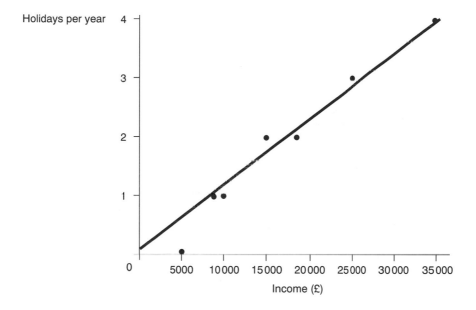

Fig. 10.7 Scattergram showing high positive correlation between income and number of holidays per year

It can be seen from the completed scattergram in Fig. 10.7 that the correlation in this case is high and positive.

In some cases it is impossible to draw a regression line between points on the scattergram, in which case there is said to be zero correlation between the variables under consideration, as in the case of Fig. 10.8.

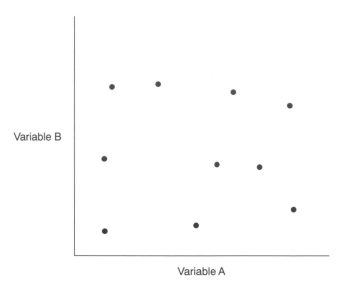

Variable B

Variable A

Fig. 10.8 Scattergram showing zero correlation between Variable A and Variable B

Self-assessment test questions

These questions have been designed to test your recall of the main points in this chapter. The answers can be found on page 222.

Complete the following sentences:

1 A pie chart can be used . . .

2 The middle values of numerical data can be examined by three measures of . . .

3 The arithmetic mean is obtained by . . .

4 The disadvantage of the arithmetic mean is that . . .

5 The mode is the most . . .

6 The median is the figure . . .

7 Time series analysis is a technique for . . .

8 The disadvantage of moving averages is that . . .

9 A 'line of best fit' is known as a . . .

10 When it is impossible to draw a 'line of best fit' between points on a scattergram, there is said to be . . .

State whether each of the following statements is TRUE or FALSE:

11 There are four measures of central tendency.

12 The disadvantage of the arithmetic mean is that it is hard to calculate.

13 The mode is the most frequently-occurring value in a series.

14 Time series analysis is based on the assumption that previous sales patterns can be used to predict future sales performance.

15 A moving average is calculated by working out four-week moving totals.

Write short notes on the following:

16 measures of central tendency

17 time series analysis

18 frequency distribution

19 correlation

20 pie charts and bar charts.

Research and discussion activity

Table 10.6 shows how disposable household income was distributed between different groups of the population in 1979 and 1991. The data shows the percentage distribution of household incomes after tax and benefits. In 1979 the percentage of total income earners was 35 per cent – in 1991 it had increased to 41 per cent.

Table 10.6   Distribution of disposable household income, 1979 & 1991

	Percentage of total disposable household income in	
	1979	*1991*
Bottom fifth of population	10	7
Second fifth of population	14	12
Middle fifth of population	18	17
Fourth fifth of population	23	23
Top fifth of population	35	41
	100	100

1   How might you arrange this information most effectively in visual form?

2   What conclusions can you draw from this data?

Now look at the graph in Fig. 10.9 which shows average weekly wages for the period 1978 to 1992. Does the graph add to your understanding of the data about the distribution of household income?

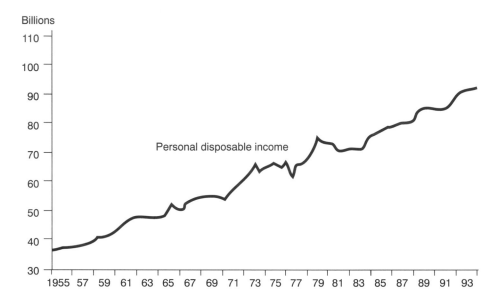

Fig. 10.9 Graph showing average weekly wages for the period 1978–1992

Market forces

After reading this chapter you should be able to:

◆ List the characteristics of the perfect market

◆ Explain what a demand schedule and a supply schedule are

◆ Explain the principal causes of changes in demand and supply

◆ Explain what is meant by elasticity of demand and supply.

So far in this book we have looked at the world of business from the marketer's perspective. In this chapter we are moving beyond the boundaries of the marketing discipline to look at some key economic concepts that marketers need to understand.

In Chapter 1 we saw that marketers use the word 'demand' to describe a customer's ability and willingness to pay for a product or service. In this chapter we shall be looking at the concept of demand from an economist's point of view. Economists define demand as follows:

> **Demand: the quantity of a product or service that purchasers will buy at a given price.**

 ## Demand and supply

Demand for a product or service means the quantity of product or service demanded at a certain price. 'Demanded' here means how much of the product or service people will want to buy, and not necessarily how much they will buy. As a general rule, the quantity demanded will increase if the price falls and decrease if the price rises.

Demand schedules and curves

A consumer's demand for a product or service varies with variations in the price charged for it. Table 11.1 shows how an individual consumer's demand for a packet of tea increases as the price of the tea falls. Consumer A is prepared to purchase one packet of tea if the price is 96p per packet, but will purchase five packets if the price falls to 70p per packet.

Table 11.1 Consumer A's demand for tea

Price of tea per packet (pence)	Quantity demanded by Consumer A
96	1
92	2
82	3
80	3
74	4
70	5

The *individual demand schedule* for Consumer B (Table 11.2), however, shows that this individual would not make a purchase until the price falls to 82p per packet, and instead of buying five packets at 70p each, Consumer B will buy only three packets.

Table 11.2 Consumer B's demand for tea

Price of tea per packet (pence)	Quantity demanded by Consumer B
96	0
92	0
82	1
80	2
74	3
70	3

A *composite demand schedule* is a theoretical combination of all the individual demand schedules for a product or service. It illustrates the total demand for the product or service at different prices. A composite demand schedule for packets of tea might look like Table 11.3.

Table 11.3   Total demand schedule for packets of tea

Price of tea per packet (pence)	Quantity demanded
96	1000
92	1000
82	2000
80	2000
74	3000
70	4000

A demand schedule can also be expressed in the form of a graph, as shown in Fig. 11.1. It is a convention in economics that the horizontal axis is marked *OX*, and the vertical axis is marked *OY*. It is also conventional to show price along the vertical axis and quantity along the horizontal axis. In Fig. 11.1 the curve shows the state of demand for packets of tea at different prices. The purpose of this graph is merely to show the general relationship between price and the quantity demanded, and so there is no need to mark off the price and quantity scales mathematically.

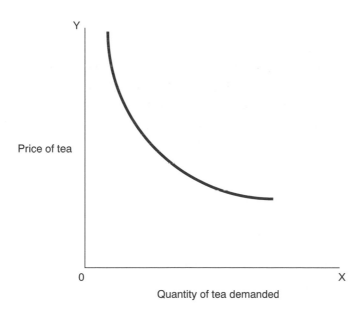

Fig. 11.1 Graph showing the relationship between price and demand of tea

Figure 11.1 illustrates the first law of supply and demand, which can be expressed in this way: the lower the price, the greater the quantity that will be demanded. Most demand curves follow the slope of the one shown in Fig. 11.1, but some exceptional demand curves slope upward from left to right, showing demand increasing as price rises, instead of decreasing. Exceptional demand curves occur in the following circumstances:

◆ The demand for some luxury goods, such as perfume, increases with increasing prices, as the product is perceived as being more desirable.

◆ Demand for a product or service may increase after a price rise if consumers think there is likely to be a further price rise in the near future. This phenomenon frequently occurs on the Stock Exchange.

◆ Cheap staple foods provide another good example of exceptional demand curves. Quantities of these foods demanded tend to remain relatively stable over quite wide price ranges. When, however, the prices of all food types are rising, the quantity of cheap staple foods demanded may increase as the prices of other foods move beyond the reach of the poorest people in society.

 ## Supply schedules and curves

In the same way that there is a relationship between demand and price, so there is a relationship between supply and price. *Supply* indicates the quantity of a product or service supplied at different prices. Once again, it is important to note that supply is a measure of the quantity of a product or service that businesses will *want* to supply at different prices, rather than a measure of how much they *will* actually supply. As a general rule, the quantity supplied will increase if the price rises and decrease if the price falls. Table 11.4 illustrates a supply schedule for tea, showing the quantities that will be put on the market at different prices.

Table 11.4 Supply schedule for tea

Price of tea per packet (pence)	Quantity supplied
96	4000
92	3500
82	3000
80	2000
74	1500
70	1000

In this example, 4000 packets of tea will be supplied if the price per packet reaches 96p per packet, but only 1000 packets will be supplied if the price falls to 70p per packet. This illustrates the second law of supply and demand, which can be expressed in this way: the higher the price, the greater the quantity that will be supplied.

A supply schedule can be represented graphically, as shown in Fig. 11.2.

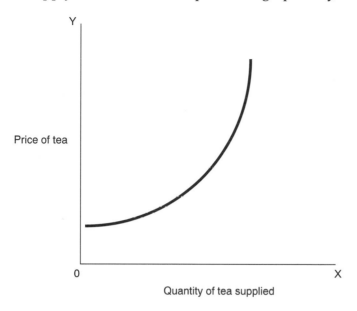

Fig. 11.2 Graph showing the relationship between price and supply of tea

Just as there are exceptional demand curves in certain circumstances, so there are exceptional supply curves, as in the following cases:

◆ The supply of some products or services is fixed because of their rarity. Works of art are examples of products falling into this category. If the supply of a product or service is fixed, a price rise will not result in an increase in the quantity supplied.

◆ The supply curve for labour may sometimes slope backwards on a portion of the curve, as a workforce is prepared to work less hours if wages are high.

 ## The equilibrium of demand and supply

The price at which demand and supply are equal is known as the *equilibrium price*. At this price the quantity demanded is equal to the quantity supplied.

The equilibrium price for packets of tea can be discovered by combining the demand and supply schedules, as shown in Table 11.5.

Table 11.5 Combined demand and supply schedules for tea

Price of tea per packet	Quantity demanded	Quantity supplied
96	1000	4000
92	1000	3500
82	2000	3000
80	**2000**	**2000**
74	3000	1500
70	4000	1000

The equilibrium price for tea in this example is therefore 80p per packet, because at this price demand and supply are both equal at 2000 packets. This information can be represented graphically, as shown in Fig. 11.3. The equilibrium price is P, at which point the quantity supplied is Q.

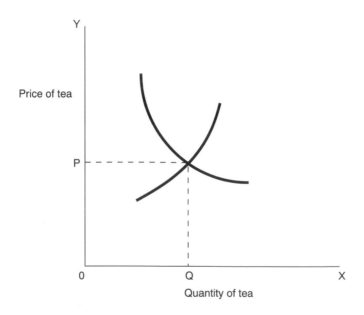

Fig. 11.3 Demand and supply curves combined to find equilibrium price

The determination of price by the interaction of demand and supply is known as the *price mechanism* and has the following important consequences:

◆ If the equilibrium price of a product is the price actually charged for the product, there will be a sufficient quantity supplied to meet demand at that price.

◆ If the market price is higher than the equilibrium price, some quantity of the product will remain unsold because customers wish to buy less than suppliers wish to make available. There is said to be an *excess of supply*.

◆ If the market price is lower than the equilibrium price, there will be a shortage of the product, as demand at that price exceeds supply.

 ## Changes in demand

It is important to note the difference between movement along a demand curve and shifts in demand. Figure 11.4 shows that the quantity of goods demanded at different prices varies according to the price at which the goods are offered. This does not mean that there are shifts in demand, but merely that there is movement along the same demand curve.

Fig. 11.4 Demand curve

In Fig. 11.5, however, demand has shifted from curve D1 to curve D2. A greater quantity of the product is now being demanded at the old prices. At the price P, demand has shifted from Q1 to Q2.

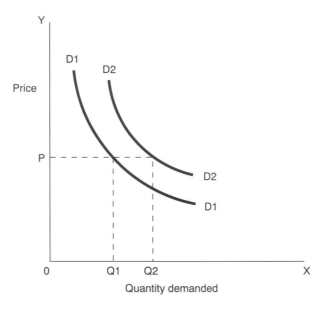

Fig. 11.5 Shift in demand illustrated by new demand curve

Changes in demand can be caused by the following events:

◆ *Increases in real income* This will usually cause an increase in demand for consumer durables and luxury goods, although the demand for basic foodstuffs and necessities remains relatively constant.

◆ *Changes in the quantity of money* This affects demand because the prices of goods do not change in the same proportions as increases or decreases in the quantity of money.

◆ *Changes in income distribution* Government action on taxes, public expenditure, and subsidies to basic foodstuffs all affect demand by redistributing income.

 ## Changes in supply

As was the case with demand, the same distinction between movements along the same supply curve and shifts in supply has to be noted. In Fig. 11.6, supply has increased at the price P from Q1 to Q2.

Changes in supply may be caused by the following events:

◆ *Changes in average costs of production* Supply tends to decrease when the cost of raw materials rises. Supply increases when technological improvements reduce average costs of production.

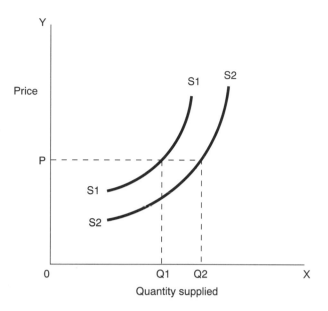

Fig. 11.6 Shift in supply illustrated by new supply curve

◆ *Agricultural output* can be affected by weather conditions, which can make it difficult to estimate production levels accurately. Supply responses to price changes in agriculture are slow because of the long period between sowing and harvesting.

◆ *Changes in taxation* A tax increase on a commodity tends to decrease supply, as it has an effect similar to that of an increase in average costs of production.

◆ *Changes in the price of commodities* When the price of certain commodities rises, producers tend to divert their resources into more profitable areas, thus causing the supply of commodities whose price has not risen to decrease.

 Consequences of changes in demand and supply

The following are some of the typical effects of changes in demand and supply:

◆ If demand increases, prices will rise in the short term as producers prepare to increase their production output to meet the increased demand. An increase in demand tends to result in both a price rise and an increase in the quantity of the product supplied.

155

◆ If demand decreases, there is a tendency for both the price of the product and the quantity supplied to decrease also.

◆ If supply increases, there is a tendency for the price to fall and for the quantity demanded to increase.

◆ If supply decreases, there is a tendency for the price to rise and the quantity demanded to decrease.

 Elasticities of demand

The *price elasticity of demand* is a measure of the responsiveness of demand to changes in the price of a product or service. If a small price change causes a large change in demand, demand is relatively *elastic*. If a large change in price has only a small effect on demand, demand is relatively *inelastic*. When elasticity of demand is greater than 1, demand is elastic. When elasticity of demand is less than 1, demand is inelastic. When elasticity of demand is equal to 1, there is said to be *unit elasticity*.

Price elasticity can be calculated using the following formula:

$$\text{Price elasticity of demand} = \frac{\% \text{ change in quantity demanded}}{\% \text{ change in price}}$$

Price elasticity of demand is affected by the following factors:

1 *Substitutes* If substitutes for a product are available, demand for the product tends to be fairly elastic, as consumers switch between products in response to price changes. When the price of apples rises, for example, consumers can choose to purchase an alternative fruit which has not risen in price.

2 *Income* The higher an individual's income, the more inelastic the individual's demand is likely to be, as price increases are not felt much. In the same way, the demand for very cheap items is generally inelastic.

3 *Habit* The demand for habit-forming goods, such as alcohol and tobacco, tends to be inelastic.

4 *Durability* The demand for durable goods tends to be fairly elastic, as consumers take advantage of price falls to make purchases of televisions or washing-machines.

Income elasticity of demand is a measure of the responsiveness of demand to changes in income. Income elasticity of demand can be calculated using the following formula:

$$Income\ elasticity\ of\ demand = \frac{\%\ change\ in\ quantity\ demanded}{\%\ change\ in\ income}$$

Cross elasticity of demand is a measure of the responsiveness of demand for one product against changes in the price of another product. Cross elasticity of demand can be calculated using the following formula:

$$Cross\ elasticity\ of\ demand = \frac{\%\ change\ in\ demand\ of\ product\ X}{\%\ change\ in\ price\ of\ product\ Y}$$

 # Elasticities of supply

Price elasticity of supply is a measure of the responsiveness of supply to changes in price. If a change in price causes a less than proportionate change in supply, then supply is relatively *inelastic*. If a change in price causes a more than proportionate change in supply, then supply is relatively *elastic*. When elasticity of supply is greater than 1, supply is elastic. When elasticity of supply is less than 1, supply is inelastic. When elasticity is equal to 1, there is said to be *unit elasticity*.

Price elasticity of supply can be calculated using the following formula:

$$Price\ elasticity\ of\ supply = \frac{\%\ change\ in\ quantity\ supplied}{\%\ change\ in\ price}$$

Price elasticity of supply is affected by the following factors:

1 *Time* The longer it takes to produce a commodity, the less responsive to price changes will be the supply of the commodity. The supply of raw materials and agricultural products tends to be inelastic.

2 *Factors of production* It is difficult to increase supply in response to an increase in price if there is a shortage in labour, land, capital or enterprise.

3 *Output* An expansion of output by existing companies, or the entry of new companies into the market, increases supply. In the same way, supply is decreased when existing companies contract their output, or when companies leave the market.

Self-assessment test questions

These questions have been designed to test your recall of the main points in this chapter. The answers can be found in on page 222.

Complete the following sentences:

1 Economists use the concept of the perfect market to . . .

2 In a perfect market, prices would be determined solely by . . .

3 Demand for a product or service means . . .

4 The first law of supply and demand is . . .

5 The second law of supply and demand is . . .

6 The price at which demand and supply are equal is known as the . . .

7 Elasticity of demand is a measure of . . .

8 Elasticity of supply is a measure of . . .

9 A composite demand schedule is a . . .

10 If demand increases, prices are likely to . . .

State whether each of the following statements is TRUE or FALSE:

11 The Stock Exchange is an example of a perfect market.

12 Economists divide consumer markets into wholesale and retail markets.

13 The price at which demand and supply are equal is known as the equilibrium price.

14 Supply responses to price changes in agriculture are speedy.

15 If supply decreases, there is a tendency for the price to fall.

Write short notes on the following:

16 the perfect market

17 exceptional demand curves

18 exceptional supply curves

19 movements along a demand curve, and shifts in demand

20 (a) income elasticity of demand

(b) cross elasticity of demand.

Discussion activity

Look at the following list of products and try to decide how demand generally might change if the price of each product was increased by 10 per cent.

◆ lap-top computer

◆ loaf of sliced bread

◆ hotel accommodation

◆ plnt of beer in a pub

◆ foreign holiday.

Now consider how the following individuals might react to the same price increase in the products:

◆ company director

◆ retired person on State pension

◆ office worker.

12 Market structures

After reading this chapter you should be able to:

◆ **List the conditions for perfect competition**

◆ **Distinguish between total, average and marginal revenue**

◆ **Distinguish between monopolistic competition and oligopoly**

◆ **Explain why a monopolist has to decrease Its price in order to increase the number of units it sells.**

We saw in Chapter 1 that, from a marketing point of view, the term 'market' refers to buyers, whereas when economists use this term, it is to refer to both buyers and sellers. Another term used by economists is 'market structure', which refers to all the characteristics of a market, such as the number of companies operating in an industry and the kinds of products made. Economists recognise four principal kinds of market structure: perfect competition, monopoly, monopolistic competition and oligopoly (see Table 12.1).

Table 12.1   Characteristics of the four principal market structures

| | *Competition* ←——————————→ *No competition* | | | |
	Perfect competition	*Monopolistic competition*	*Oligopoly*	*Monopoly*
Suppliers	infinite	many	few	one
Differentiation	none	some	significant	total
Market information	perfect	imperfect	imperfect	perfect
Entry barriers	none	few	some	high

160

Perfect competition

Economists use the concept of the perfect market to make the analysis of economic activity easier. It is important to remember that the perfect market is only a theoretical concept, although some markets in the real world come close to meeting its conditions. A perfect market would have the following characteristics:

◆ a large number of buyers and sellers, so that the market for a product or service is not influenced by the actions of any individual buyer or seller

◆ homogeneity of the product or service, which means that all products are the same, so that a buyer may make a purchase from any of the sellers

◆ close contact between buyers and sellers so that changes in the supply or demand for the product or service are known to all participants in the market

◆ free movement into and out of the market, so that people can decide when to commence trading and when to cease trading in the product or service

◆ no preferential treatment in the form of discounts or duties imposed on purchases or sales.

In a perfect market, prices would be determined solely by the interaction of supply and demand. Companies operating in such a market would be 'price takers' in the sense that price would be set by market forces. In the real world, however, markets do not have the characteristics described above, as these examples show:

◆ The retail market is not perfect because buyers are not in close contact with each other and often fail to make purchases at the lowest price because they do not know which retail outlets have the best offer. Furthermore, buyers frequently make purchases at a retail outlet for reasons other than price, for example out of habit or for convenience.

◆ The market in houses is imperfect because houses cannot be transported from one part of the country to another.

◆ The Stock Exchange is not a perfect market because knowledge of the present price of shares is not enough to justify the decision to purchase or sell them.

◆ Any market which is subject to government intervention in the form of import duties, taxes or subsidies is thereby made imperfect.

One important theoretical consequence of perfect competition is that the demand curve for an individual company would be perfectly elastic. This is because the output of a single company would never be great enough to affect the output of the total industry and thus demand. The demand curve would therefore be horizontal, as is shown in Fig. 12.1.

Fig. 12.1 Demand curve for company in perfect competition

Another important consequence of perfect competition is its effect on different kinds of revenue. Economists distinguish between the following kinds of revenue:

1 *Total revenue* is the sum received by the seller from the sale of a product. Total revenue (TR) is calculated by the following formula:

$$TR = price \times number\ of\ products\ sold$$

2 *Average revenue* is the amount of revenue received per unit sold. Average revenue (AR) can be calculated by the following formula:

$$AR = price\ per\ unit\ of\ product$$

3 *Marginal revenue* is a measure of the change in a company's total revenue when one unit of product is changed. Marginal revenue (MR) can be calculated by the following formula:

$$MR = \frac{change\ in\ revenue}{change\ in\ output}$$

Table 12.2 shows how these different revenue concepts can be applied to an imaginary company operating in conditions of perfect competition.

Table 12.2   Total, average and marginal revenues of company in perfect competition

Units	Price	TR	AR	MR
20	7.00	140	7.00	–
21	7.00	147	7.00	7.00
22	7.00	154	7.00	7.00
23	7.00	161	7.00	7.00
24	7.00	168	7.00	7.00
25	7.00	175	7.00	7.00

In conditions of perfect competition, in which the output of an individual company does not affect price, marginal revenue, average revenue and price are equal.

 # Monopoly

The opposite situation to perfect competition is monopoly. A monopoly occurs when the output of an entire industry is controlled by one company. Unlike a company operating in conditions of perfect competition, a monopoly is a 'price maker'. This means that it has the power to set a market price for its products. Monopolies have the following characteristics:

◆ there are no other suppliers in the industry, and so the relative strength of the company is great

◆ a single-product monopoly is highly differentiated

◆ monopoly prices are known and communicated easily to customers

◆ there are very high entry barriers to the industry, often supported by legislation preventing other companies from competing.

We saw that the demand curve facing an individual company in perfect competition is horizontal because it can sell any quantity of products that it has the capacity to make at the market price. The situation for a monopoly, however, is different. A monopoly is the only supplier in an industry. A monopolist's demand curve, therefore, is equal to the demand curve for the industry as a whole (see Fig. 12.2). It was shown in Chapter 11 that demand for a product has a negative slope, as people wish to buy less as the price rises and more when the price falls.

Average revenue, for a monopoly which charges the same price for all its units of production, is equal to price. The negative slope of the demand curve means that a monopolist has to decrease its price in order to increase the number of units it sells. This feature of a monopoly has an important consequence for marginal revenue. Consider the monopolist's demand curve in Fig. 12.2. In Fig. 12.3, price is decreased from P1 to P2. The effect of this decrease is that sales increase from Q1 to Q2.

Fig. 12.2 Demand curve for a monopoly

Although total revenue is increased, the marginal revenue from each extra unit sold declines because the price charged for all units has been reduced. Table 12.3 illustrates this.

Table 12.3 Effect of reducing price on marginal revenue for a monopoly

Units	Price/AR	TR	MR
20	7.00	140.00	–
21	6.90	144.90	4.90
22	6.80	149.60	4.70
23	6.70	154.10	4.50
24	6.60	158.40	4.30
25	6.50	162.50	4.10

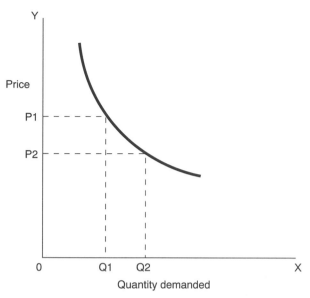

Fig. 12.3 Effect of price decrease on demand for a monopoly

GET READY FOR D-DAY

You will know them by the bags under their eyes. At the quadrennial telecommunications trade show running in Germany until October the 10th, they'll be there by the planeload, representing Europe's public telephone companies, the so-called PTT's. And if their motto in Geneva appears to be eat, drink and be merry, for tomorrow we die, forgive them: they may well be right. New Year's Day of 1998 will be upon them before they know it.

No industry today is in greater flux than telecommunications. It was once a stable business, almost a tedious one. It involved stringing copper wires from one place to another, so that people could talk over them. The company would then collect strictly regulated fees. Now in the United States, the United Kingdom, and most recently Sweden, the business has become maddeningly complex, brutally competitive, and stripped of all certainty. On January 1, 1998, the same will happen in the rest of Europe if, as planned, Brussels drops the continent's regulatory barriers to entry. For Europe's telecom companies, it is D-day: D for deregulation, with an invasion of rich, new entrants riding a flood tide of technological change.

The companies most plainly at risk are the 14 European national phone monopolies. By both history and habit, they are in most cases nothing more than public utilities – the lone gatekeepers to local and long-distance telephone service. That is all they have ever been – and it shows. They are oblivious to market pressures, charging unreasonably high prices for business connections and long-distance calls simply because the regulators will allow it. They are unresponsive. Deutsche Telekom can still take two weeks in parts of East Berlin to get a new phone line into an apartment. 'Sometimes it seems as if their slogan is "The customer is always wrong",' says Berliner Chris Ettlinger.

Newsweek, 16 October 1995

A special kind of monopoly can be formed by all the suppliers in an industry agreeing to limit their output to the level that maximises their joint profits. This is called a *cartel*. Each member of the cartel is then allocated an output quota. If all the participants in the cartel limit their output to the allocated quota level, and there are no new entrants to the industry, an effective monopoly is created.

Imperfect competition

Most companies do not operate either in conditions of perfect competition or monopoly. Economists use the term 'imperfect competition' to describe these market structures.

We saw that companies in perfect competition sell the same product as each other, and that they are 'price takers'. The great majority of companies in imperfect competition, however, sell differentiated products. This means that each company must also select a price for its products, thus becoming a 'price maker'. A company in imperfect competition does not respond to short-term fluctuations in demand by changing its prices, as a company in perfect competition would be forced to do. Instead, fluctuations in demand are met by changing levels of output. Two further characteristics of companies in imperfect competition are important. The first is that they use advertising and promotion to attract both new customers to the market and existing customers away from competitors. This kind of rivalry between companies is known as *non-price competition*. Second, they often try to prevent other companies from entering the market by erecting *entry barriers* to the industry.

Economists distinguish between two forms of imperfect competition: monopolistic competition and oligopoly. We will look at each in turn.

Monopolistic competition

The economic theory of monopolistic competition is based on the following assumptions:

◆ each company produces one type or brand of an industry's differentiated product, which means that an individual company's demand curve is negatively sloped and highly elastic because of the existence of substitute products

◆ there are so many companies in the industry that each one ignores the reactions of the others when making decisions about price and production levels

◆ the industry has no entry and exit barriers; demand for the industry is shared between all producers

◆ there is symmetry, which means that new entrants take their share of the market from all existing companies in equal measure.

According to the theory of monopolistic competition, individual companies can make a profit in the same way that monopolies do in the short-run. This is because each company produces a differentiated product. However, the theory also states that when profits are being made, new entrants will join the industry and the demand curve for each company will shift to the left. This leads to an apparently paradoxical situation, known as the *excess capacity theorem*. In monopolistic competition each company is forced to produce less than its full capacity, and its average costs of production are higher than they need to be.

In recent years economists have argued that the theory of monopolistic competition does not reflect modern business conditions. This is because most industries are not made up of many companies, each of which produces just one variant of the industry's product. It is more accurate to say that most industries are dominated by just a few companies, each of which makes a range of differentiated products. Economists use the term *oligopoly* to describe this situation.

Oligopoly

An oligopoly exists when an industry is dominated by a small number of suppliers, such as the high street banks in Britain or international airline companies. Each company is sufficiently powerful to be a price maker, but it also faces a number of important competitors. An oligopolist's competitors are small enough in number to respond to any of its actions, and relations between companies are therefore said to be *strategic*. This means that an oligopolist, unlike companies in perfect competition, cannot make pricing decisions solely by reference to its own costs and demand curve; the reactions of competitors also have to be taken into account. This market structure has the following characteristics:

◆ there are few suppliers in the industry, or the industry is dominated by a few suppliers, although some much smaller companies also operate in the market

◆ there is a significant degree of product or service differentiation

◆ companies engage in non-price competition against each other

◆ there are some entry barriers to the industry, including the following:

Economies of scale These occur when a company with many customers can manufacture products more cheaply than smaller competitors through the use of automated production processes.

Economies of scope These occur when a company with many customers can develop new products more cheaply than smaller competitors, because the fixed costs of new product development are spread over greater sales.

Economists argue that companies operating in conditions of oligopoly have two fundamentally opposing strategies from which to choose. The first is to co-operate with each other, in which case all the companies in the industry act together to reduce inter-company rivalry: this co-operation results in an effective monopoly being formed. Explicit agreements between companies to set common prices for the industry's output are illegal in most countries, although it frequently happens that companies working in the same industry set prices within tacitly agreed ranges for similar products.

BOOKSELLERS FEAR SAD ENDING

Europe's booksellers and publishers fear small bookshops and publishing houses may face closure if the collapse of the UK's book price-fixing arrangement spreads to the rest of the continent.

Roland Ulmer, chairman of the German Publishers and Booksellers Association, said this week that the decision by large UK publishers to withdraw from the country's century-old net book agreement 'fills booksellers and publishers in other countries with alarm'. Ulmer was speaking at Frankfurt's annual Book Fair – the largest in the world.

The agreement is still formally in existence – and will remain so until the UK's Office of Fair Trading rules otherwise – but since major publishers such as Pearson, Harper Collins and Random House have withdrawn in order to remain competitive, observers believe that it is only a matter of time before it disappears.

The European, 12–18 October 1995

The second strategy for companies in oligopolistic industries is for each company to seek to pursue its own interests at the expense of other companies. We saw in Chapter 7 that companies constantly monitor their competitors' actions in an attempt to predict their behaviour. Economists argue that this kind of 'strategic' behaviour is a feature of oligopolistic industries.

Self-assessment test questions

These questions have been designed to test your recall of the main points in this chapter. The answers can be found on page 223.

Complete the following sentences:

1 In a perfect market prices would be determined by . . .

2 The retail market is not perfect because . . .

3 The demand curve for an individual company in perfect competition would be . . .

4 A monopolist's demand curve is equal to the demand curve for . . .

5 Non-price competition is . . .

6 An oligopoly exists when an industry is . . .

7 Economies of scale occur when . . .

8 Economies of scope occur when . . .

9 A cartel occurs when . . .

10 Economists argue that strategic behaviour is a feature of . . .

State whether each of the following statements is TRUE or FALSE:

11 Economists recognise four principal kinds of market structure.

12 In a perfect market companies would be 'price makers'.

13 Total revenue is the sum received by the seller from the sale of a product.

14 Average revenue is a measure of the change in a company's total revenue when one unit of production is changed.

15 In conditions of imperfect competition, fluctuations in demand are met by changing price levels.

Write short notes on the following:

16 perfect competition

17 monopoly

18 monopolistic competition

19 oligopoly

20 total, average and marginal revenue.

Discussion activity

Does the privatisation of nationalised industries always lead to greater competition and efficiency?

Business-to-business marketing

After reading this chapter you should be able to:

◆ List the three ways in which consumer and organisational markets differ from each other

◆ Describe what is meant by 'derived demand'

◆ Distinguish between producer, reseller, government and institutional markets

◆ List the principal roles that members of a decision-making unit may have

◆ Distinguish between buy-phases and buy-classes.

In Chapter 2 we looked at some of the factors which influence consumer purchase behaviour. In this chapter we turn our attention to organisational purchasing. We will first give a classification of industrial markets and the kinds of products and services that are most commonly purchased. Then we will discuss the structure and functions of buying centres, and examine the process of organisational buying.

It is more common nowadays to use the term 'business-to-business' marketing to describe the marketing activities which take place between organisations, rather than the terms 'industrial marketing' or 'organisational marketing'.

Differences between consumer markets and organisational markets

The three main differences between consumer markets and organisational markets concern market structure, the way companies approach their customers, and the buying process.

Market structures in organisational markets tend to be very concentrated, with a relatively small number of customers being responsible for a substantial percentage of sales. Purchases also tend to have very high unit values in comparison with purchases in consumer markets.

Another important difference between consumer markets and industrial markets is that demand in industrial markets is a derived demand, i.e. that it is derived from consumer demand. There is little that organisational producers can do to stimulate consumer demand directly, but companies should still monitor consumer trends on a regular basis.

Increases in consumer demand for particular products have little effect on the demand for capital equipment, at least in the short term. This is because it is nearly always possible to respond to such increases by increasing capacity. In the same way, a decrease in consumer demand can be met by removing plants from service, or by reducing planned levels of plant replacement.

Demand for specific industrial outputs, however, can be affected by changes in the level of consumer demand for finished products.

The demand for organisational goods is sometimes cyclical, characterised by periods of activity which accompany economic growth, followed by periods of relative tranquility. Organisational markets are also characterised by reciprocal selling, when suppliers agree to purchase goods from each other.

In industrial markets products tend to be sold directly to the final user, and there is great emphasis on product demonstrations, technical advice and after-sales service.

 ## Organisational markets

There are four principal classifications of organisational market. These are producer markets, reseller markets, government markets and institutional markets. We will look at each of these in turn.

1 *Producer markets* are those in which goods are purchased which will either be used to make products or be sold to consumers. These types of goods include machine tools and components for radios.

2 *Reseller markets* are those in which goods and services are purchased by distributors for resale to consumers. As we saw in Chapter 2, many producers do not sell their products directly to consumers but employ intermediaries for this function.

3 *Government markets* are ones in which goods are sold to local or central government. The government is a major purchaser of defence equipment, as well as having requirements for road-building and hospital equipment. There has been a movement in recent years for traditional government purchase decisions to be made the responsibility of specialist agencies or 'trusts'. Some government purchasing is therefore similar to purchasing in institutional markets.

4 *Institutional and public sector markets* are ones in which the principal concern is the provision of some kind of social or other service. Examples of these markets include prisons, universities and charities. Institutional and public sector purchasing tends to be organised by publicising the organisation's requirements, and requesting interested suppliers to submit a tender. Three kinds of tender procedure are widely used:

(a) *Open tendering* occurs when the organisation makes a very public invitation to tender.

(b) *Selective tendering* occurs when the organisation invites bids from selected suppliers only.

(c) *Private contracting* occurs when the organisation makes contact with one or more suppliers individually.

The degree of discretion which an organisation in the public sector has in the awarding of tenders varies:

◆ *Automatic tendering* occurs when the organisation must award the contract either to the lowest bidder or on the basis of some other, predetermined criterion.

◆ *Discretionary tendering* occurs when the organisation can accept the bid which is most advantageous to the buying department, on the basis of predetermined criteria.

◆ *Negotiated tendering* occurs when the organisation negotiates the conditions of the contract, in the way that a private sector company would.

Industrial products and services

The following list demonstrates the range of goods and products purchased by organisations:

1 *Capital equipment* This category of industrial goods includes all the plant and machinery which a company needs to carry on production. Although price is an important factor in the purchase decision of capital

equipment, other factors are also of critical importance, such as technical sales advice and support, spare parts availability and after-sales service.

2 *Accessories* This category of industrial goods includes secondary capital items such as office equipment, ancillary plant equipment and maintenance. Accessories are less expensive than capital equipment, and their importance to the basic function of the company is less central.

3 *Raw materials* The purchase of the raw materials which make up part of the final product is usually the most costly element in a purchasing department's total procurement. Sometimes the final product is a consumer product, but often it is an industrial product. As we shall see, the purchase of raw materials must take account not only of price, but also of quality, delivery, continuity of supply and level of service.

4 *Component parts and materials* These are similar to raw materials, in that they make up part of the final product. As with raw materials, price is not usually the sole consideration of purchasers.

5 *Supplies* This category of industrial goods includes all the routine expenditure of a company on stationery, cleaning materials and other small items. The purchase decision for supplies is usually routine, and price is likely to be a determining feature.

6 *Services* Industrial services include management consultants, external marketing agencies, and other services such as contract cleaners. The decision on whether to use outside service providers usually depends on their cost-effectiveness.

R W Cooper and P D Jackson have noted the following differences between consumer products and industrial products:

◆ there are fewer purchasers for industrial products, which are more technical than consumer products

◆ order quantities for industrial products are larger

◆ demand for industrial products is derived

◆ industrial products are used for many purposes

◆ technical service, both before and after purchase, is very important for industrial products

◆ product packaging for industrial products is not promotional

◆ competition for industrial products is frequently on the basis of specification and delivery reliability, rather than price alone.

Buying centres

The principal difference between organisational purchase decisions and consumer purchase decisions, is that organisational purchasing is usually the result of a group decision. It is very rare for one individual in a company to have total responsibility for all the decisions involved in making a purchase. The group of people involved in making a company purchase decision is called a decision-making unit or *buying centre*.

There has been a lot of research into the nature and dynamics of buying centres. Specifically, research has focused on the following questions:

◆ How many people take part in a buying centre?

◆ Who are they?

◆ What are their roles?

The size of a buying centre can vary from as few as three to as many as 40 people, depending on the complexity of the purchase decision to be made. The complexity and importance of the purchase decision also determines who becomes involved in the purchasing process: top management are likely to be less closely involved in routine buying decisions than in the purchase of very complex or important equipment. A study by F E Webster and Y Wind in 1972 suggested that members of buying centres have the following roles:

1 *Users* These are people in the organisation who will be the users of the product or service to be bought. Users are likely to be more concerned with product performance and ease of use than with price, and so it is important for suppliers to maintain contact with the users of their products.

2 *Buyers* These are people in the organisation who have a formal responsibility to make purchases. We discussed some of the factors in the relationship between buyers and suppliers in Chapter 4 in our discussion of stakeholder relationships. The status given to buyers within an organisation can vary enormously. In some companies the buyer simply processes decisions made by others, whereas in others the buyer contributes greatly to the purchase decision. Suppliers need to understand the relative importance of buyers in each of the organisations to which they sell.

3 *Influencers* This category includes anyone who influences the purchase decision, either directly or indirectly, by giving information to the buying centre. Influencers may be people in the company or they may be outside it.

4 *Deciders* These are the people in the organisation who have a formal responsibility for taking purchase decisions. They are likely to be members of senior management, whose involvement in purchasing is usually limited to policy-making.

5 *Gatekeepers* These are the people in the organisation who control the flow of information to and from the members of the buying centre.

Purchase situations

The complexity of a specific purchase situation depends on the experience and technical knowledge of a company and not on the purchase itself. Three *buy-classes* have been identified. These are:

1 *New buy* This occurs when the company has no previous experience of the product or supplier. This is the most complex purchase situation, and senior management are likely to be involved in the purchase decision-making process.

2 *Modified re-buy* This occurs when the company has some experience of the product or supplier, but some details of the purchase situation have changed. The product specifications may have been modified since the last purchase, for example, or it may have been decided to change supplier.

3 *Straight re-buy* This is the simplest purchase situation, in which routine re-ordering relies on decisions taken in the past.

The organisational buying process

It is generally agreed that the fundamental process of organisational buying involves the following stages:

1 *Need recognition* This occurs when a company recognises that it has a need which can be met through the purchase of a product or service.

2 *Determination of specifications* The company prepares a general, and then a very specific, description of the product or service it wishes to purchase.

3 *Information search* In this stage of the purchasing process the company seeks to acquire information about the product or service. Sources of information used include specialist publications, trade journals, buyers in other companies, trade shows and contacts with sales personnel.

4 *Evaluation of alternatives* In this stage the company evaluates both a range of products or services and a range of potential suppliers.

5 *Selection* The company makes its final choice of product and supplier.

6 *Post-purchase evaluation* The company identifies any problems that have arisen since the purchase.

Many models of the organisational buying process have been proposed. Some of the most important of these include:

Task models

These models of organisational buyer behaviour assume that the desire for rational outcomes influences purchase behaviour, and task models therefore stress such factors as costs, rational economics and purchase management.

Non-task-related models

These models emphasise the non-task-related outcomes of individuals participating in the purchase process. Non-task-related outcomes include ego enhancement or personal gain, buyer/colleague relationships, and the desire to avoid risk in purchase decisions.

Complex models

A model proposed by P Robinson and others in 1967 linked the concept of 'buy-classes' to 'buy-phases'. This model is shown in Table 13.1.

Table 13.1 Buy-classes and buy-phases model

Buy-phases	Buy-classes		
	New task	Modified re-buy	Straight re-buy
Identification of need	X	X	X
Determination of requirement	X	n/a	n/a
Specific description of requirement	X	n/a	n/a
Search for potential sources	X	n/a	n/a
Examination of sources	X	n/a	n/a
Selection of sources	X	X	X
Order routine established	X	X	n/a
Evaluation of performance feedback	X	X	X

n/a = not applicable

J N Sheth's model of organisational buying behaviour, which is shown in Fig. 13.1, provides a dynamic interpretation of organisational buying behaviour.

The model emphasises the following variables:

◆ *Psychological factors* which can distort the perceptions of members of the buying centre. These include education, role, lifestyle, previous experience and expectations.

◆ *Decision-making* which, Sheth argues, is either autonomous or jointly executed. Joint decision-making results in conflict between buying centre members, which is resolved through problem solving, persuasion, bargaining or 'politicking'.

◆ *Situational factors* which, Sheth argues, interrupt the decision-making process. Examples of situational factors include the economic environment, industrial problems or promotional efforts.

Another complex model of organisational buying behaviour is that of F E Webster and Y Wind, shown in Fig. 13.2.

This model concentrates on the role of the individual decision-maker in the buying centre and on the effects of the following variables:

◆ environmental determinants of buying behaviour

◆ organisational determinants of buying behaviour

◆ interpersonal determinants of buying behaviour

◆ individual participants.

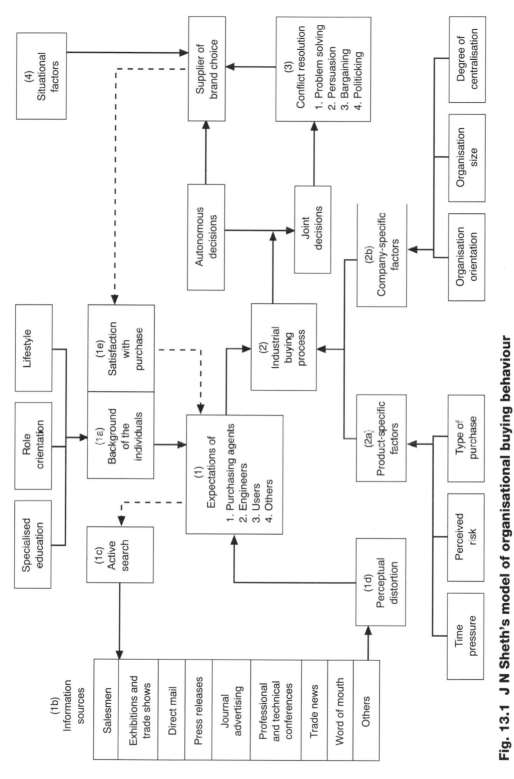

Fig. 13.1 J N Sheth's model of organisational buying behaviour

Source: J N Sheth, 'A model of industrial buying behaviour', *Journal of Marketing*, 37(4), October, 1973

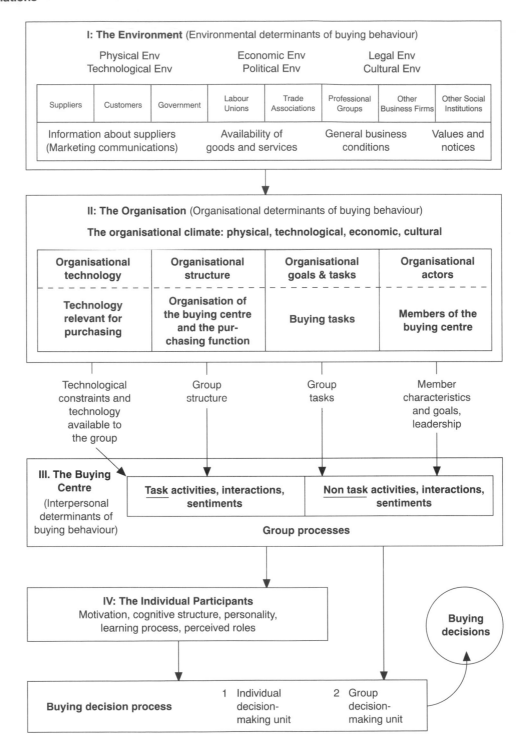

Fig. 13.2 Webster and Wind's model of organisational buying behaviour
Source: W Webster and Y Wind, *Organisational Buying Behaviour*, Prentice-Hall, Englewood Cliffs, NJ, 1972

Self-assessment test questions

These questions have been designed to test your recall of the main points in this chapter. The answers can be found in on page 223.

Complete the following sentences:

1 The three main differences between consumer and organisational markets concern . . .

2 Producer markets are those in which . . .

3 Reseller markets are those in which . . .

4 The group of people involved in making a company purchase is called a . . .

5 A new buy occurs when . . .

6 A modified re-buy occurs when . . .

7 A straight re-buy occurs when . . .

8 Task models of organisational behaviour assume that . . .

9 Non-task-related models emphasise . . .

10 J N Sheth's model of organisational purchasing stresses . . .

State whether each of the following statements is TRUE or FALSE:

11 Market structures in organisational markets tend not to be concentrated.

12 There are three principal classifications of industrial market.

13 The decision whether to use outside service providers is usually taken by reference to costs.

14 The size of a buying centre can vary from 10 to 50 people.

15 Gatekeepers are people who control the flow of information to members of a buying centre.

Write short notes on the following:

16 the classification of organisational markets

17 the range of goods and services purchased by organisations

18 buying centres

19 buy-classes

20 the organisational buying process.

Research activity

Use the weekend edition of your local newspaper to discover the products and services your local authority is putting out to tender. How are bids to be submitted?

Strategies

After reading this chapter you should be able to:

◆ Distinguish between a mission statement and corporate objectives

◆ Describe what is meant by situational analysis

◆ List the four product/market strategies identified by I Ansoff

◆ Distinguish between penetration pricing, price skimming, product-line pricing and early cash recovery pricing

◆ List the main elements in annual plan control and efficiency control.

In his book *Marketing Management*, P Kotler describes the current business environment as 'turbulent', and expressions of this turbulence are not hard to find. The last twenty years have seen the rise of new technologies, an increase in the globalisation of trade, and widespread anxieties on the part of consumers and governments about the physical environment.

Another cause of turbulence in the business environment has been the tendency of large businesses to grow in size, with the consequence that competition has also increased.

All this means that businesses need to formulate strategic plans rather than relying on ad hoc judgements or an intuitive 'feel' about the future. Nowhere is this more true than in marketing departments if they are to contribute fully to the achievement of organisational goals and objectives.

 ## Mission statement

A corporate mission statement is a senior management decision about the company's current and future purposes, which is expressed in general

terms. We have already seen, in T Levitt's famous example about American film-makers, that it is important to define a company's fundamental purpose in terms of customer needs as well as in terms of products. A mission statement takes account of the company's strengths and weaknesses and seeks to answer the following key questions:

◆ What kind of business is the company in?

◆ What kind of business does the company want to be in, and by when?

◆ What is the company's current financial position, and what is it projected to be in the future?

◆ Who are the company's customers? What are their needs?

◆ What are the company's technologies?

Although decisions about the mission statement are usually taken by senior management, and are therefore 'top-down' decisions, they cannot be made without information and assistance from lower down the company hierarchy. 'Bottom-up' data will come from the production and finance departments, as well as the marketing department.

 ## Objectives

Corporate objectives follow on from the mission statement and set out the dates by which certain objectives should have been reached. Corporate objectives are about setting targets, not the means to reach them. Typical corporate objectives relate to the following:

◆ market position

◆ return on investment

◆ asset growth

◆ productivity.

 ## Situational analysis

Having set out the corporate mission statement and expressed this in terms of clear objectives to be attained by fixed dates, the next phase in the marketing planning process is to carry out a detailed marketing audit. As we saw in Chapters 1 and 3, a marketing audit consists of an examination of the company's external and internal environments.

The purpose of the external audit is to analyse trends in the PEST factors discussed in Chapter 3. It is also necessary, as part of the external audit, to carry out a market and competition profile. A typical checklist for this part of the situational analysis will consider the following:

◆ total market size and trends; market shares of main competitors and competing brands; seasonal and regional variations

◆ customer analysis; purchase timing, location and frequency rates; reasons for purchase; brand and advertising recall

◆ competitor and competitor product identification; competitor product strengths and innovations

◆ product benefits and quality compared with competition costs and prices; packaging and design; product alternatives and substitutes; product developments and innovations

◆ distribution channel analysis; number and types of intermediaries used; relative strengths of distributors and retailers.

In the internal audit the company carries out an in-depth examination of its marketing performance, concentrating on sales analysis, market share, and the profitability of individual products.

The external and internal audits can be represented in a SWOT format, which, as we saw in Chapter 3, allows a company to match internal strengths with external opportunities and convert internal weaknesses where these may be opposed by external threats.

Marketing objectives, strategies and tactics

It is important to distinguish between marketing objectives, strategies and tactics.

◆ *Marketing objectives* are derived from corporate objectives. They are statements of what is to be achieved.

◆ *Marketing strategies* are statements of how objectives will be achieved.

◆ *Marketing tactics* are specific action plans designed to achieve marketing strategies.

M McDonald has argued that an ineffective marketing strategy invariably brings decline to a company. The relationship between strategy and operations is illustrated in the matrix in Fig. 14.1.

MARKETING OPERATIONS

	Ineffective	Effective
Efficient	Company fortunes decline slowly	Company thrives and grows
Inefficient	Company fortunes decline rapidly	Company survives

MARKETING STRATEGY

Fig. 14.1 Relationship between strategy and operations

SWOT analysis provides information about a company's environment, competitors, and internal strengths and weaknesses. This information is used to clarify the assumptions on which the time scale of the marketing plan can be based. Many companies combine an annual marketing plan with a five-year plan. This rolling plan principle ensures that plans are always focused on the future but subject to regular control.

It is important to remember that, whereas general marketing objectives are drawn from corporate objectives, specific marketing strategies are indicated by the SWOT analysis.

 ## Strategies for growth

I Ansoff has identified four generic product/market strategies from which a company can choose. They are illustrated in Fig. 14.2.

1   *Market penetration* consists of concentrating on the company's range of existing products. The intention is to increase sales, by attracting new customers, by persuading existing customers to make more frequent purchases, or by taking customers away from competitors.

Product Market	Present	New
Present	**1** Market penetration	**3** Product development
New	**2** Market development	**4** Diversification

Fig. 14.2 Ansoff matrix identifying four gonorio produot/morkct strategies

2 *Market development* consists of offering existing products to new customer groups. This strategy is becoming increasingly popular with European companies as trade between member states is facilitated by the European Union.

3 *Product development* consists of offering existing customers modified or new products, taking advantage of an established customer base.

4 *Diversification* consists of finding new customers and making new products available. It is the most risky of the four strategies identified by I Ansoff, although rewards are correspondingly high when the strategy is successful.

Having formulated the marketing strategy, the next phase of strategic marketing is to implement the plan. This involves identifying the tasks to be carried out and the personnel responsible for them, as well as establishing a monitoring system. It also involves drawing up contingency measures which can be applied if there are major environmental changes which necessitate modifications to the chosen direction of the marketing plan.

FULL STEAM AHEAD

Carnival Cruise Line makes boatloads of money by selling fun

Chuck Whitman, 38, almost won the hairy-chest contest. Marie Johnson, 64, played the slots and left with pockets jingling. Robin and Cedric Braatz, both 23, got married in the library and then danced the night away in the Neon Bar. Honeymooners Tracy and Steve Meraw, 26, snorkeled in Key West and stole kisses in the Mayan ruins of Cozumel. And Tyson Gray, 7, wore the mask he made in the children's parade.

All were on ecstasy two weeks ago – the boat, that is – one of the splashy Carnival Cruise Line 'Fun Ships' that Katie Lee Gifford has been giddily crooning about for more than a decade. When it pulled into the Port of Miami after four days in the Gulf of Mexico, its 2200 passengers – many packing Mexican tapestries and straw hats – seemed sated and satisfied. It had drizzled for two of those days, but most didn't mind. After all, on a Fun Ship, rain is just God's way of saying it's time to head for the karaoke bar.

Floating resort

No, this is not the QE2. A Carnival cruise is a gaudy affair, a big, ten-storey floating resort with bright lights, loud colours, dancing girls and Devin Fleming, your cruise director, who's busy hunting Elvis impersonators for amateur night. Carnival's corporate captains, ever mindful that Las Vegas attracts 28 million visitors a year that way, aren't proud. They have created the biggest and most profitable cruise line in the world by throwing stuffy old seafaring conventions overboard and giving mainstream Americans what they want: hassle-free fun, sun, glitz, games, all the roast tenderloin and grilled salmon they can eat, baby sitters, even free air fare – delivered in one-price-covers-everything packages averaging about $207 a day.

At the helm is Micky Arison, 46, chairman and CEO of the Carnival Corp, which just rang in its 15th straight quarter of record profits.

With revenues of $1.8 billion and earnings of $382 million last year, Carnival, which operates 22 ships on four different cruise lines, is far and away the leader of the rapidly expanding cruise industry. Like his recently retired father, Ted, an Israeli immigrant who started the company in 1972 with a revamped freighter featuring vaudeville acts and skeet shooting, Micky Arison has relied chiefly upon a simple growth strategy. Build it, make it splashy, and they will come. 'We went from being bottom feeders to Number One in ten years,' declares the younger Arison, who credits his father's vision of a cruise ship as a destination unto itself and shrewd, consistent marketing to middle-class travellers as the keys to Carnival's success. Indeed Arison spent $90 million on advertising and promotion last year. 'Carnival's strong brand identification far surpasses everyone else in the cruise industry,' explains Paul Mackey, an analyst at Dean Witter. 'All of the other lines have much fuzzier images.'

Arison's cruise ships are certainly packing them in. Carnival has been operating at 100 per cent of capacity for several years, whereas the industry average has hovered at about 85 per cent. With business so strong, Carnival has aggressive expansion plans. Over the next four years, the company plans to build eight more ships at a cost of $2.5 billion. Carnival's major rivals have responded the only way they can, by building equally large boats with just as many bells and whistles. Royal Caribbean, Carnival's closest competitor, is adding five new superliners to its fleet of nine ships in the next three years, while Princess Cruise Lines, also with nine ships, is adding two more 'Love Boats' in 1997, one with 2600 berths. As a result, industrywide capacity will increase more than 40 per cent by 1998. With 30 ships, and a solid balance sheet, Carnival should command one third of the market.

US News & World Report, October 16 1995

The implementation of a marketing plan follows the selection of one of the four strategies described. It is usual to develop specific programmes for each of the four elements of the marketing mix: product, price, promotion and place.

 ## Product strategies

Product strategies must be consistent with a company's overall objectives, and they need to take into account both the strengths and weaknesses of the company, and the opportunities and threats of the external environment. Specific product decisions involve the following:

1 *Product items* Most companies offer more than one product item, and decisions have to be taken about product item features, packaging, design and branding.

2 *The product line* Most companies offer products which are similar to each other in certain respects, and decisions have to be taken regarding how many products in the same line to maintain: too few products in a line reduces customer choice, and too many increases costs. Decisions also have to be taken regarding the timing of new products and the phasing out of older ones from the same line.

3 *The product mix* This refers to the number of product lines offered by a company and the number of product items within each line. Product mix *depth* is a measure of the number of items in a given line; *width* is a measure of the number of lines in the product mix.

 ## Pricing strategies

1 *Penetration pricing* consists of offering a product at a low enough price to encourage customers to buy it. It is a strategy followed by companies introducing a new product onto the market who want to establish market share. Sometimes a company will introduce a new product with this price strategy, hoping to be able to raise prices once a customer base has been established. Frequently, however, resorting to a higher price at a later stage of the product life-cycle means that customers will seek alternative products.

Penetration pricing works only when competitors cannot compete with the penetration price. If they can compete, a 'price war' is the likely consequence, as happens periodically in the British newspaper industry.

2 *Price skimming* consists of offering a product at a high price to capture specific market segments. It is a strategy followed by companies introducing a new product onto the market who want to recoup development costs quickly. After 'skimming' these higher-paying market segments, the price of the product is lowered to attract more price-sensitive segments. This pricing strategy is successful in markets with high entry barriers which prevent competitors from offering lower-priced alternatives.

3 *Product-line pricing* consists of examining the relationship between a company's related products and offering these at different prices. A coffee manufacturer, for example, might offer one instant coffee product at a low price to appeal to certain buyers, and another instant coffee at a higher price to appeal to different buyers.

4 *Early cash recovery pricing* consists of offering a product at a price which will produce profit in the short term rather than in the long term. It is a strategy followed by companies who do not believe in the long-term market for their product, or who require an immediate cash return. The strategy works by combining the market skimming and market penetration strategies, according to the prevailing conditions of the market.

Promotion strategies

For now it is enough to understand that company promotion is concerned with communications between a company and its different stakeholder groups. There are four elements in the promotional mix: advertising, publicity, sales promotion and personal selling.

There are two basic promotional strategies from which a company can choose. These are:

1 *Pull strategy* This consists of encouraging consumer demand for a product through the intense use of advertising and promotion. The success of the pull strategy depends on having the product readily available in retail outlets. The launch of Microsoft's 'Windows '95' was accompanied by a pull strategy.

2 *Push strategy* This is the opposite to the pull strategy. A company selecting a push strategy does not invest heavily in consumer advertising or promotion, but focuses its efforts on retail outlets and sales personnel. The intention is to achieve success through the promotion and selling effort of intermediaries.

Place strategies

P R Cateora has suggested that there are five strategic goals to be achieved from a distribution strategy. These are the five C's of distribution: cost, control, coverage, character and continuity. We will look at each of these in turn.

1 *Cost* Decisions with regard to cost are focused on the capital cost of establishing and maintaining a distribution channel, and the costs of establishing a sales force. Many companies prefer to avoid the expense of establishing their own distribution channels and rely instead on the services of marketing channel intermediaries, a subject discussed in Chapter 2.

2 *Control* A company with its own sales force has maximum control over the distribution of its products, but the costs of these are sometimes prohibitive.

3 *Coverage* The concept of coverage refers to the capacity of the marketing channel to meet all members of the target market, as well as its capacity to carry all of a company's products. Some distributors are unwilling to take responsibility for all of a company's product lines, and it may be necessary to establish a company sales force for these.

4 *Character* The character of a distribution channel refers to the 'fit' between a company and its markets. Arranging such a fit can sometimes be a problem, and it may be necessary either to compromise on company standards or to leave certain markets if adequate intermediaries cannot be found.

5 *Continuity* A distribution system's continuity refers to its capacity for consistency. As we saw in Chapter 2, independent intermediaries often perceive themselves as having different interests to manufacturers, and this can mean that it is difficult to achieve continuity.

In Chapter 2 we saw that the fundamental distribution strategies are:

◆ *intensive distribution*, in which a company seeks to make its products available in the maximum number of retail outlets

◆ *selective distribution*, in which a company seeks to make its products available only in profitable outlets, or outlets whose image will not damage company reputation

◆ *exclusive distribution*, in which a company seeks to make its products available only in limited outlets, in order to enhance the prestige of the product.

HOW PIRELLI PULLED OFF A 180-DEGREE TURN

When Marco Tronchetti Provera needs a break from running Italian tire and cable giant, Pirelli, he leaves his Milan office and heads for the Cauris, the 18-meter sloop he keeps moored in Portofino. His closest friends say Tronchetti's real nature comes out when he and his crew are in a tight race. 'Despite the tension, he never loses his cool,' says one sailing buddy. 'You'll never see him lose his temper or shout.'

That is how Tronchetti runs Pirelli. Since taking the helm of the company in 1992, just as it was reeling from a foiled raid on Germany's Continental Tire, the soft-spoken Tronchetti has quietly steered Pirelli from near-bankruptcy to strength. In September, Pirelli reported a doubling of net profits in the first six months of 1995, to $70 million, and about a 20% sales increase, to $3.5 billion. While Italy's weak lira helped boost Pirelli's exports and market share, analysts give most of the credit for the transformation to Tronchetti's three-year shakeup. Tronchetti, says Italy analyst Mike Peciti of London's James Capel Inc, 'has done an exceptional job of turning Pirelli around.'

Tronchetti's strategy has been to refocus management strength on Pirelli's core businesses. 'If you manage mature businesses well, you can make money,' he says. Now, after five years of heavy losses, Pirelli is finally earning money in tire sales. Having cleaned up the act in Europe, Tronchetti wants to improve results at troubled New Haven-based Armstrong Tire Corp, which Pirelli bought in 1988. New managers despatched last May have orders to make the unit break even by 1997.

After becoming CEO, Tronchetti lost no time house-cleaning. He set up a new management team, and they worked overtime to unload dozens of companies Pirelli had acquired in the 1960s and 1970s in a feverish bid to diversify out of its maturing tire and cable markets. Tronchetti orchestrated a fire sale of properties, ranging from sneaker factories to apparel units to big chunks of downtown Milan real estate, halving the group's $2.5 billion debt load and cutting the workforce by 25% to 39 000.

Meanwhile, Tronchetti is working to boost market share. He is concentrating on high-performance tires, the fastest growing and most profitable segment of the European tire market. Originally meant for sports cars, the low and wide tires now make up about 25% of all European tire sales, with Pirelli leading in the segment. Its new P6000 tire has been a runaway success and was accepted by 11 car manufacturers in Europe. Overall, Pirelli is No. 2 in Europe after Michelin, with 12% of the market.

In cables, which account for about half of Pirelli's $6.5 billion in sales, Tronchetti is repositioning the group as a major telecommunications player. Already neck and neck with Alcatel Alsthom as top international supplier of fiber optic cable, Pirelli is researching technology to vastly increase the amount of data that can be transmitted with such cables.

What's next? There's some talk in Milan financial circles that Pirelli could spin off its revitalised tire division to raise money for further moves in higher-growth telecom. For now, Tronchetti says he aims to expand the tire business into East Asia, where it has been weak. But if a suitor comes along, analysts suggest, he may ignore old industrial traditions and steer Pirelli through yet another dramatic turn.

Business Week, 16 October 1995

Competitive strategies

In Chapters 2 and 7 we discussed the three competitive strategies identified by M E Porter: cost leadership, differentiation and focus. In Chapter 7 we also discussed the concept of market followers and niche markets.

Marketing plan control

It is important to build into a strategic marketing plan a system of controls by means of which a company can evaluate its marketing activities. An effective system of controls depends on three elements:

◆ establishing clear performance standards, which need to be flexible because environmental forces may result in changes to corporate objectives

◆ evaluating marketing performance by reference to the established standards

◆ taking corrective action when performance does not meet planned levels.

We will examine three types of marketing control: profitability control, annual plan control and efficiency control.

Profitability control

As well as measuring the profitability of individual products, sales regions and specific consumer groups, profitability control is used to assess the performance of marketing activities. Marketing profitability control identifies those market costs which are attributable to the principal marketing activities of packaging, distributing, advertising and selling. A profit-and-loss statement for each of these activities is then prepared, in order to identify areas where corrective action may be required. This can be a difficult process because it is necessary to decide the basis on which costs should be applied to each of these activities. Three kinds of costs are involved:

1 *Direct costs* include the salaries and other costs of marketing personnel, and also the costs of advertising and promotion which can be related to specific products.

2 *Traceable common costs* include those costs which cannot be directly assigned to marketing activities, such as the cost of company premises.

3 *Non-traceable common costs* are costs whose allocation to marketing are somewhat arbitrary, such as expenditure on company image, taxes, interest payments and other costs. Some companies do attribute these costs to marketing, following what is called the 'full-cost' approach. Others do not attribute such costs to marketing on the grounds that to do so would be to confuse accounting for financial reporting with accounting for decision-making and long-term planning.

 ## Annual plan control

Annual plan control is designed to assess the extent to which a company has achieved planned sales levels. Annual plan control is usually carried out by senior and middle management. To be successful, annual plan control requires a commitment to four steps. First, the company should set monthly or quarterly achievement goals. Second, market performance should be monitored carefully. Third, serious performance problems should be identified. Finally, the company should be prepared either to change its achievement targets or to take corrective action where there is a discrepancy between its planned levels of achievement and its actual performance. Annual plan control is used to evaluate performance in any of the following areas:

1 *Sales analysis* is a technique for measuring sales performance against planned targets. It analyses sales levels by reference to company divisions or product groups, customer groups, products and brands, and members of the sales force. The advantage of sales analysis is that it is relatively easy to apply. Its principal disadvantages are that it takes no account of the fact that sales figures can rise or fall because of environmental factors beyond the control of the company.

2 *Market share analysis* looks at a company's performance within the total market or compares it against the performance of its chief competitors. As we saw in Chapter 7, market share analysis can be expressed in terms of volume of sales, value of sales, or as a comparison against competitors.

3 *Marketing expense to sales analysis* is designed to control a company's expenses in the following areas: the sales force, advertising, sales promotion, and sales administration.

4 *Financial analysis* is designed to measure a company's rate of return on net worth. It takes account of the following factors: profit margin, asset turnover, return on assets, and financial leverage.

5 *Customer attitude analysis* is used to assess the likelihood of major changes in consumer attitudes which may affect the company's future market share. Customer attitude analysis is the only qualitative method used in annual plan control. Customer attitudes can be obtained from the following sources: customer complaints, consumer panels and consumer surveys.

 Efficiency control

Profitability control can indicate that a company's profits are lower than they should be with regard to one or more marketing activities. Efficiency control can then be used to gauge the efficiency of those activities. This technique can be applied to the sales force, advertising, sales promotion and to distribution.

When applied to the sales force, efficiency control takes account of the following indicators of sales force efficiency:

◆ average number of sales per salesperson per day

◆ average sales call time per product

◆ average revenue per sales call

◆ average cost per sales call

◆ entertainment cost per sales call

◆ percentage of orders per one hundred sales calls

◆ number of new customers per period

◆ number of lost customers per period

◆ sales force cost as a percentage of total sales.

When applied to advertising, efficiency control takes account of the following factors:

◆ advertising costs per thousand buyers

◆ percentage of total audience with advertising recall

◆ consumer opinions on advertising content and effectiveness

◆ number of product enquiries stimulated by advertising

◆ cost per enquiry.

When applied to sales promotion, efficiency control takes account of the following factors:

◆ percentage of sales made under promotion terms

◆ display costs per pound of sales

◆ percentage of promotion coupons redeemed

◆ number of product enquiries resulting from promotions and displays.

Efficiency control can also be applied to distribution systems, with models to improve inventory control, the siting of warehouses, and the organisation of transportation systems.

Self-assessment test questions

These questions have been designed to test your recall of the main points in this chapter. The answers can be found on page 224.

Complete the following sentences:

1 Businesses need to formulate strategic plans rather than rely on . . .

2 Decisions about the mission statement are usually taken by . . .

3 The purpose of corporate objectives is to . . .

4 A marketing audit consists of an examination of . . .

5 Marketing strategies are statements of . . .

6 Marketing tactics are specific action plans designed to . . .

7 The Ansoff matrix identifies four . . .

8 Marketing profitability control is used to . . .

9 Annual plan control is used to . . .

10 Efficiency control is used to . . .

State whether each of the following statements is TRUE or FALSE:

11 A mission statement is expressed in general terms.

12 Marketing objectives are derived from marketing tactics.

13 Market development consists of concentrating on existing customers.

14 Penetration pricing consists of offering a product at a low price.

15 Marketing plan control depends on three elements.

Write short notes on the following:

16 mission statement

17 corporate objectives

18 marketing objectives, strategies and tactics

19 the Ansoff matrix

20 product strategies.

Group activity

Look at the press articles included in this chapter. What strategies have these companies followed?

Market segmentation

After reading this chapter you should be able to:

◆ List the four criteria necessary for successful market segmentation

◆ Distinguish between undifferentiated, differentiated and concentrated marketing

◆ List the most common forms of demographic segmentation

◆ Explain the principal characteristics of the ACORN system

◆ Explain what is meant by psychographic and lifestyle segmentation.

We have made a distinction between the production approach to business and the marketing approach. It has been said that a company with a marketing approach seeks to ensure its own profitability by giving customers a range of products or services which satisfy their needs and wants. Not all of a company's potential customers have the same needs and wants. It is therefore important to sort potential customers into groups, each group having its own defined needs and wants. *Market segmentation* consists of identifying groups of customers with differing needs.

In order for a market segment to be of value to a company it must meet four criteria. First, the segment must be *identifiable*. That is, it must be a distinct part of the market and different from other parts. Next, it must be *quantifiable* and sufficiently large to justify company investment in it. A segment which is unquantifiable, or one which is too small to justify investment in it, is of no value to a company. Third, a segment must be *accessible*. A company must be able to reach the segment with its promotional messages and to distribute the product effectively and efficiently.

Finally, a segment must be *relevant* to a company's resources, skills and objectives.

As well as contributing to profitability, market segmentation has a number of other advantages for a company. A company which perceives its customers as belonging to groups with diverse needs and wants is in a position to react quickly and sensitively to changes in customer requirements. It is also possible for such a company to become the product leader in certain market segments, benefiting from its specialist knowledge.

The process whereby a company selects which segments of the market it will serve is known as *targeting*. For the present it is sufficient to outline broadly the four targeting strategies available to a company.

1 *Mass marketing* Also called undifferentiated marketing, this strategy consists of offering the same product to all segments of the market. Undifferentiated marketing allows a company to benefit from the economies of scale which result from mass production. Many companies which used to follow the undifferentiated approach have now expanded their range of products in order to serve distinct segments. Coca-Cola, for example, which was originally available in one flavour only, is now available in different forms to suit the different tastes of the company's millions of customers.

2 *Differentiated marketing* This strategy involves offering the same product to different segments, but varying the promotional mix for each segment served. The variations in promotional mix focus on the needs and wants of each segment. A good example of differentiated marketing is provided by Barbour jackets. These jackets are marketed as traditional countrywear in certain parts of England and as urban fashion items throughout the European market.

3 *Differentiated target marketing* This strategy consists of offering different products to different segments. In differentiated target marketing the promotional mix is also varied to focus on the needs and wants of each segment. An obvious example of this kind of marketing occurs in the car industry, where a range of models is offered to meet the requirements of different segments.

4 *Concentrated marketing* Also called niche marketing, this consists of offering a product to a single segment of the market. Concentrated marketing has a particular appeal for small companies which lack the resources to serve the whole market or many segments. This strategy allows a company to develop a very close relationship with its customers.

Examples of concentrated marketing include specialist boat-builders and shops which sell bridal clothes.

There are many criteria by which potential customers can be divided into groups. It is important to remember that the following bases are not used in isolation. They are generally combined with one another to provide detailed information about a segment or segments. The process of combination is illustrated in Figs. 15.1 and 15.2.

In Fig. 15.1 the market has been segmented according to income groups. In Fig. 15.2 income group 1 has been further segmented into age groups.

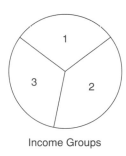

Income Groups

Fig. 15.1 Market segmentation according to income groups

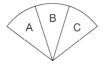

Income Group 1 segmented into Age Groups

Fig. 15.2 Further segmentation into age groups

 # Demographic segmentation

Every ten years the government carries out a Census of the Population of Great Britain. Many companies use census data as the basis for their own demographic analyses of the population. Demographic segmentation consists of dividing the market by reference to one or more of the following criteria:

Age

Many products are targeted at specific age groups. The fashion industry, for example, provides different products for customers of different ages. The music industry also serves customers of varying age segments: chart music is aimed at younger customers; whereas 'easy listening' products are aimed at older people.

Sex

Often the market is segmented according to gender, as is the case with clothing and toiletry products. Other product examples include magazines intended primarily for women and sporting goods for use by men. It is sometimes important for a company to know not only the gender of the purchaser of a product but also the gender of the user.

Income

The market can be segmented according to the income of customers. Cars, holidays and other products are very often targeted at specific income groups.

Education level

It is common to segment the market for certain products according to education levels. Books, newspapers and magazines are frequently targeted in this way. Companies adapt their product advertisements according to the assumed education level of the target market.

Social class

Although segmentation by social class is still practised by some companies, the concept of social class has changed so much in recent times that there is considerable debate over the usefulness and relevance of traditional social class groupings. Furthermore, traditional class groupings take almost no account of changing family structures and the role of women in the economy. The most common method used is the one developed by the National Readership Survey (NRS). This classification system divides the population into six social classes:

A: Upper Middle Class This class forms 3 per cent of the population. It comprises people with inherited wealth and others in the most senior professional, managerial and administrative positions. Representatives of this class include barristers, bishops, brain surgeons and leading business people. The upper class enjoys rich and luxurious lifestyles.

B: Middle Class   This class forms 10 per cent of the population. It comprises people in professional, managerial or administrative careers who have not yet achieved the highest positions. Middle class people are described as having comfortable, but not luxurious, lifestyles.

C1: Lower Middle Class   This class forms 24 per cent of the population. It comprises people in junior managerial, supervisory or administrative positions and 'white-collar' workers. Lower middle class people have a lifestyle considerably lower than that of middle class people.

C2: Skilled Working Class   This class forms 30 per cent of the population. It comprises skilled workers, such as electricians and plumbers. Members of this class frequently have a greater income than some members of the lower middle class.

D: Working Class   This class consists of semi-skilled or unskilled manual workers, and includes factory operatives and farm labourers, as well as unskilled workers in service industries.

E: The Poor   This class consists of unemployed people and pensioners who live at the lowest levels of subsistence.

 ## Family life-cycle

The family life-cycle is a demographic tool which segments the market according to various stages in family development. The family life-cycle indicates not only the kinds of products consumers are likely to buy at different phases of the cycle, but also variations in disposable income.

 ## Geo-demographic segmentation

Dissatisfaction with traditional social class groupings, such as that of the NRS discussed previously, has led to the development of different segmentation methods which have a greater accuracy in predicting consumer purchase behaviour.

One of the most successful of the new methods works by combining geographic and demographic factors. A Classification Of Residential Neighbourhoods (ACORN) was originally developed by Richard Webber in the late 1970s from data contained in the 1971 national census. Succeeding versions have relied on later census data.

ACORN is based on the principle that certain types of neighbourhood not only have similar housing, but also have populations with similar demographic and social characteristics. Neighbourhood populations will therefore share similar lifestyles and purchase behaviour. The ACORN system recognises eleven neighbourhood types:

A Agricultural areas

B Modern family housing

C Older housing of intermediate status

D Older terraced housing

E Council estates 1

F Council estates 2

G Council estates 3

H Multi-racial urban areas

I High-status non-family areas

J Affluent suburban housing

K Better-off retirement areas.

The ACORN system has been linked with the postal code system to provide an identification for every address in the UK. The new system, which is called MOSAIC, has been used to segment markets for many products, including food, financial services and cars.

 ## Geographic segmentation

Although geographic segmentation is considered by some analysts as being under the demographic heading, it makes sense to consider it separately. This kind of segmentation is of obvious importance in international marketing, but it is also relevant to single countries.

In the UK, geographic segmentation has traditionally been centred on regional studies. Differences in economic conditions between Scotland, the north of England and the south, suggest variations in consumption patterns for many types of products and services.

 ## Psychographic and lifestyle segmentation

Psychographics is concerned with classifying people according to personality traits. It is difficult to explain consumer purchase decisions in terms of personality traits alone, and in recent years psychographics has been combined with the study of lifestyles. Thus a connection is made between psychological factors and specific purchase decisions.

The market research company, Taylor Nelson, has carried out a series of empirical studies from which it has been able to identify three general social value groups and, within these, a further seven social value segments.

1 *Inner-directed groups*

   (a) *Self-explorers* This group forms 16 per cent of the population. Self-explorers are motivated by self-expression and self-realisation. They are not overtly materialistic and tend to be tolerant of others.

   (b) *Social resisters* This group forms 11 per cent of the population. Social resisters are motivated by fairness and quality of life. They may be dogmatic and intolerant.

   (c) *Experimentalists* This group forms 14 per cent of the population. Experimentalists are motivated by pleasure. They are highly individualistic and materialistic and frequently reject traditional authority.

2 *Outer-directed groups*

   (a) *Belongers* This group forms 18 per cent of the population. Belongers are conservative and family-centred people. They are savers rather than short-term pleasure seekers.

   (b) *Conspicuous consumers* This group forms 19 per cent of the population. Conspicuous consumers are materialistic and conservative. They are motivated by acquisition and competition.

3 *Sustenance-driven groups*

   (a) *Survivors* This group forms 16 per cent of the population. Survivors are hard-working and conservative. They have a strong community spirit and are motivated by the need to keep going.

   (b) *Aimless* This group forms 5 per cent of the population. The aimless are often young and unemployed people and are motivated by short-term pleasure. The older members of this group tend to be motivated by day-to-day existence.

BREAKING WITH TRADITION
by Flora Hunter

One of Britain's oldest fine jewellers, which has supplied the aristocracy for generations, is inviting homosexual couples to buy 'commitment rings' as a way of cementing their relationships.

Hennell in New Bond Street, established in 1736, is advertising the rings in magazines with a picture of a homosexual couple by the controversial American photographer Richard Avedon.

Hennell originally designed the rings in response to the flagging popularity of marriage, offering all couples a way of making a less formal commitment. However, when the advertising agency Beand MC suggested expanding the concept to include homosexual men, the shop's owner was enthusiastic.

Stanley Lester, a senior buyer, explained: 'Fewer people are getting married, and so fewer people are buying engagement rings, wedding bands, anniversary rings and all that goes with marriage, so we needed to find something that would fill that gap. This is a ring for anyone – some people are buying them as engagement rings, but they are also buying them for other reasons.'

The Sunday Telegraph, 1 October 1995

Reproduced by permission

Benefit segmentation

Benefit segmentation focuses on the criteria by which a potential consumer evaluates a product or service. A father buying a dinghy for his son may be interested, above all, in the product's safety features. In such a case the benefit is clearly identifiable and the company may choose to target an 'anxious father' segment of the market. The same company may target other benefit segments, either by making different products available, or by emphasising the different benefits available from the same product.

User/usage status

This kind of segmentation sorts consumers according to the frequency with which they use a product: customers can be divided into 'heavy', 'light' and 'non-user' segments.

Occasions for purchase

The purchase of some products can be linked to specific occasions, and segmentation can focus on such occasions. The purchase of toys, for example, can be linked to birthdays and to Christmas. The purchase of jewellery can be similarly linked to important family events: engagements, wedding anniversaries, and so on.

Loyalty status

This is a measure of consumer loyalty to particular brands or to particular retail outlets. The identification of segments with varying degrees of brand or outlet loyalty is important because 'loyal' consumers are unlikely to abandon their chosen brand or outlet.

Self-assessment test questions

These questions have been designed to test your recall of the main points in the chapter. The answers can be found on page 224.

Complete the following sentences:

1 The four criteria necessary for successful market segmentation are . . .

2 Market segmentation consists of . . .

3 Demographic segmentation consists of . . .

4 Traditional social class groupings take no account of . . .

5 The family life-cycle is a demographic tool which . . .

6 ACORN is based on the principle that . . .

7 In the UK, geographic segmentation has traditionally been centred on . . .

8 Psychographics is concerned with classifying people according to . . .

9 The three social value groups identified by Taylor Nelson are . . .

10 Benefit segmentation focuses on . . .

State whether each of the following statements is TRUE or FALSE:

11 Market segmentation consists of identifying customers who have different needs.

12 A national census is carried out every twenty years.

13 The National Readership Survey divides the population into ten social classes.

14 Geographic segmentation is mainly used in international marketing.

15 Benefit segmentation focuses on the customer's financial status.

Write short notes on the following:

16 the reasons why companies segment markets

17 demographic segmentation

18 the NRS system of social class groupings

19 the family life-cycle.

 ## Discussion activity

Look at the following list of publications:

◆ Cosmopolitan

◆ Yachting Monthly

◆ Tatler

◆ Financial Times

◆ Readers' Digest.

1 How would you define the readership for each publication?

2 Which of the segmentation bases you have studied in this chapter are particularly relevant to each publication?

16 International marketing

After reading this chapter you should be able to:

◆ **Understand the importance of the product life-cycle to international marketers**

◆ **Distinguish between tariff and non-tariff barriers to trade**

◆ **Describe the four basic types of national economy**

◆ **Describe the screening process of foreign markets**

◆ **List the five ways in which a company can enter a foreign market.**

It is appropriate to finish this book with a discussion of international marketing and to give a brief outline of the scope of international marketing activities and decisions.

There is some disagreement over whether the terms 'international marketing' and 'exporting' should be regarded as separate activities. Some analysts define exporting as a short-run, sales-driven activity which does not involve a customer orientation, and it should therefore not be confused with genuine marketing activity, which is more customer-focused.

Most analysts are agreed that international marketing should follow the ordinary procedures of marketing and that it therefore does not differ from domestic marketing in its fundamental approach. There are, however, some specific problems associated with moving goods and services across national frontiers, and these need to be addressed by companies.

Reasons for exporting

One of the traditional reasons given for exporting is the phenomenon of the international product life-cycle. Once a product has gone through the phases of the product life-cycle in the domestic market, the theory is that it can be introduced into foreign markets and thus go through the cycle once more (see Fig. 16.1).

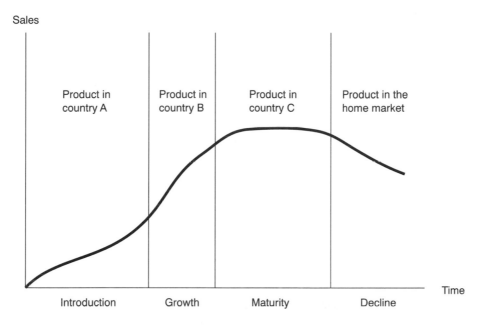

Fig. 16.1 International product life-cycle

In the current business environment, however, international competition means that the product life-cycle 'time-lag' between countries is shortening. Neither can the international product life-cycle protect companies from re-exports, as many American companies have discovered to their cost in recent years. The re-export threat can be summarised as follows:

◆ American companies develop and export high-technology products to foreign markets.

◆ Companies in the foreign markets to which the high-technology products are exported begin to make cheaper, substitute copies of the original products. They are able to make their product versions cheaper because of savings in research and development and because of lower labour costs. Gradually, their products reduce the size of the American exporting companies' overseas markets.

◆ Foreign companies, having developed economies of scale because of the demand for their products in existing markets, prepare to export their cheaper versions of American products to the American market.

◆ The American market finds itself flooded with cheaper, high-technology products from the foreign country.

M E Porter has suggested that companies may be motivated to become involved in foreign markets for any of the following reasons:

1 Currents driving international competition, such as:

◆ countries becoming more similar to each other, sharing features like large retail chains, television advertising and the use of credit cards

◆ declining tariff barriers

◆ reduction of geographical barriers due to technological advances in communications.

2 Cross-currents which have changed the pattern of international trade, such as:

◆ declining rates of economic growth

◆ changes in the basis of comparative advantage

◆ new forms of protectionism such as government requirements about the local ownership of industry

◆ new kinds of government inducements to foreign companies

◆ joint ventures involving a greater degree of collaboration than in the past

◆ new technologies which allow both for globalisation and customised products.

 ## Researching international markets

A company contemplating exporting its products has to familiarise itself with that country's PEST factors i.e. politics, economics, society and technology. We will look at each of these areas in turn.

Politics

We saw in our discussion of the macro-environment in Chapter 3 that government actions are a major influence on business. Factors which need to be considered by exporters are the following:

1 *Government stability and structure*

2 *Government bureaucracy and administration* It is important to know how efficiently government departments are run, and whether there is a local tradition of 'gift-giving' to officials.

3 *Tariffs* These are taxes on products crossing a national frontier. These may be imposed to raise government revenue or to protect domestic industries.

4 *Non-tariff barriers are any form of government action designed to restrict imports* A quota is a limit set on the amount or value of a product that a country will allow to be imported. Other forms of non-tariff barrier include customs, administrative or technical policies designed to reduce imports. Some countries have defined their national product standards in such a way as to make it almost impossible for foreign companies to enter the market.

Economics

Economists recognise four basic types of national economy.

1 A subsistence economy is one in which there is a high concentration on agriculture, and most output is consumed by the domestic market. Countries in this category include Ethiopia and Bangladesh. The opportunities for exporters in such an economy are limited.

2 A developing economy is one in which there exists a wealth of raw materials which are exported. Countries in this category include Nigeria and Mexico. There are opportunities for exporters of mining equipment.

3 An industrialising economy is one in which manufacturing accounts for 10–20 per cent of the country's gross national product. Countries in this category include the majority of South American countries. There are opportunities here for exporters of industrial raw materials, and there may also be limited opportunities for luxury products designed for members of the wealthy industrial class.

4 An industrial economy is one in which selected raw materials are imported, and manufactured goods are exported. Countries in this category include Japan and most West European states. This kind of economy provides the widest range of opportunities for exporters of all product types.

Society

1 *Language problems* Even within the European Union, where English is the accepted language of international business, linguistic problems can arise in the translation of documents, and in contract negotiations. This is particularly the case with regard to the interpretation of legal matters, because of the different systems of law in use. Other language problems arise with choosing product names, and the design of advertisements.

2 *Customs* It is important for the international marketer to understand the customs of those countries where it is intended to do business. National customs affect both the way that business is conducted, and the kinds of products for which there is likely to be demand.

 ## The research process

The research process remains essentially the same as that outlined in Chapters 8 and 9. In general, research for international marketing should begin with initial screening of markets of potential interest. The purpose of initial screening is to determine the following:

1 *Market accessibility* This consists of examining whether tariffs, non-tariff barriers to trade or quota systems are in operation in any of the proposed markets.

2 *Consideration of profitability* This part of the research process is concerned with establishing the following:

 ◆ Current market potential, which is obtained by studying total industry sales in the market.

 ◆ Market potential forecast, which is obtained by predicting how future economic and political events will affect the market.

 ◆ Sales potential forecast, which is obtained by predicting the company's future market share.

 ◆ Forecast of cost and profits, which is obtained by subtracting estimated costs from estimated profits.

 ◆ Estimate of return on investment.

It is usual to conclude the initial screening of potential foreign markets by giving each one a rating.

 ◆ *'A' markets* are those with the best opportunities in the short and long term.

◆ *'B' markets* are attractive but have some characteristics which are perceived as disadvantageous. Investment in 'B' markets will be more cautiously undertaken than investment in 'A' markets.

◆ *'C' markets* are less attractive still but may have some potential for limited investment.

Useful sources of secondary data for the initial screening of foreign markets include:

◆ British Overseas Trade Board (BOTB)

◆ European Union (EU)

◆ Economic Commission for Africa (ECA)

◆ Economic Commission for Asia and the Far East (ECAFE)

◆ Economic Commission for Latin America (ECLA)

◆ Organisation for Economic Co-operation and Development (OECD)

◆ General Agreement on Tariffs and Trade (GATT)

◆ World Trade Information Service.

Once markets of potential interest have been identified through initial screening, it is important to follow up with field research on the markets concerned. Field research can be carried out either by the company itself or an agency.

 ## Entering a foreign market

If the results of the analysis previously described are positive, the next consideration is the best mode of entry to the market. There are five ways in which a company can enter a foreign market:

1 *Indirect exporting* This is the least risky way of entering a foreign market, and for that reason it is favoured by most companies in the first instance. Indirect exporting involves a collaboration between the exporting company and intermediaries. This collaboration can be organised in any of the following ways:

   (a) A *domestic-based export merchant* is an independent entity which buys and sells products on its own account.

   (b) A *domestic-based export agent* sells products in foreign markets on commission.

(c) A *co-operative organisation* exports to foreign markets on behalf of client producers.

(d) An *export management company* takes responsibility for all of a company's export activities.

2 *Direct exporting* This is a strategy that carries a greater degree of risk than indirect exporting. A company following this strategy must either establish an overseas sales branch or subsidiary, or employ overseas sales staff or distributors and agents.

3 *Licensing* This is an arrangement with a foreign agent or company, where the agent or company acts as licensee on its own behalf. The advantage of this strategy for the exporting company is that the licensee takes the majority of risk. Its principal disadvantage is that the exporting company loses some of its control over the selling process.

4 *Joint venture* This is a form of agreement between companies or investors to create a business in the foreign market which is jointly owned and managed. Joint ventures can involve a high degree of risk if the partners fall out over the way the venture should be controlled.

5 *Direct investment* This is the riskiest mode of entry into a foreign market in which the exporting company establishes its own foreign-based assembly or manufacturing plants. The advantages of direct exporting are that it results in the exporting company

◆ retaining full control over foreign operations

◆ developing good relations with government officials in the country

◆ building long-term relationships with local suppliers and distributors.

 ## International marketing mix decisions

A company which operates in foreign markets must determine whether it is going to adapt its products, promotional strategies and prices in order to gain a stronger foothold in the foreign market. Some companies make considerable adaptations, whereas others follow a standardised marketing mix for all markets.

Perhaps the best examples of product adaptations are to be found in the food industry. It is common for the largest manufacturers to modify their leading products to take account of different food tastes and preferences. Companies which manufacture electronic products, on the other hand, rarely modify their product offerings in this way.

There has been a considerable debate over whether companies should adapt their promotional strategies to reflect differences within the foreign markets they serve, or whether it is better to follow, as far as possible, a 'global' communications strategy. Whichever approach is followed, differences in language and local culture and customs are bound to affect promotional decisions.

Where international marketers are concerned, there may be difficulties in pricing a product according to the needs and requirements of foreign markets. Pricing strategies can be influenced by world prices, by prices in adjacent markets, and by legal and currency considerations. Generally, exporting companies can choose from one of three principal pricing methods:

◆ uniform pricing for all markets

◆ market-based pricing for each country

◆ cost-based pricing for each country.

A company can organise its international marketing activities in several ways. Perhaps the simplest, and therefore the one that is favoured by companies exporting for the first time, is to establish an export department. An export department can either take responsibility solely for foreign sales, or for foreign advertising and promotion as well.

Companies which are involved in several foreign markets frequently establish an international division which has overall responsibility for overseas activities. International divisions can be structured according to product type, according to the foreign markets they serve, or by reference to the responsibilities they have for specific international subsidiaries.

Self-assessment test questions

These questions have been designed to test your recall of the main points in this chapter. The answers can be found on page 225.

Complete the following sentences:

1 A company contemplating exporting its products has to familiarise itself with that country's . . .

2 Tariffs are . . .

3 Non-tariff barriers are . . .

4 A subsistence economy is one in which . . .

5 A developing economy is one in which . . .

6 An industrialising economy is one in which . . .

7 An industrial economy is one in which . . .

8 'A' markets are those with the best opportunities in . . .

9 'B' markets are attractive but have some . . .

10 'C' markets may have potential for . . .

State whether each of the following statements is TRUE or FALSE:

11 Most analysts believe that special procedures are required for international marketing.

12 Tariffs are taxes on products crossing national frontiers.

13 Indirect exporting is the most risky way of entering a foreign market.

14 A joint venture is a form of agreement between companies or investors to create a jointly-owned business.

15 Exporting companies can choose from five principal pricing strategies.

Write short notes on the following:

16 the international product life-cycle

17 tariffs and non-tariff barriers to trade

18 screening of foreign markets

19 modes of entry to foreign markets

20 international marketing decisions.

Discussion activity

You have been asked by a company which produces high-technology medical equipment for advice on markets in the following countries:

a) China

b) Japan

c) Germany

Without researching the countries in detail, make a list of the problems you would expect to encounter under the following headings:

a) politics

b) culture and language

c) legal and financial structures.

Answers to self-assessment test questions

Chapter 1

1 . . . that there are two or more parties to the exchange, that each party has something of value to bring to the exchange, and that the exchange is voluntary.
2 . . . the use of money, the rise of specialist skills, and the emergence of merchants or 'middlemen'.
3 . . . to make enough products to satisfy demand.
4 . . . that the supply of goods was outstripping demand.
5 . . . the management view that success is achieved through producing goods of optimum quality and cost.
6 . . . the management view that effective selling and promotion are the keys to success.
7 . . . the management process which identifies, anticipates and supplies customer requirements efficiently and profitably.
8 . . . to analyse, plan and control marketing activities.
9 . . . a separate manager accountable to the marketing director.
10 . . . different markets, regions or customers.
11 True
12 False
13 False
14 False
15 True

Chapter 2

1 . . . it contains entities outside the company's control.
2 . . . 'that which the customer buys', rather than 'what the organisation makes'.
3 . . . services.
4 . . . many sellers competing on equal terms for customers.
5 . . . there are no intermediaries.
6 . . . intensive, selective and exclusive distribution.
7 . . . channel members are separate legal entities with different interests.
8 . . . one channel member is given leadership status by the other channel members.
9 . . . a consumer's family, friends, work colleagues and other close associates.
10 . . . motivation, perception, learning processes and attitudes.
11 True
12 False
13 False

14   False
15   False

Chapter 3

1   . . . a country's political and legal system.
2   . . . it gives no indication of the relationship between a country's wealth and its population.
3   . . . fundamental beliefs, attitudes, values, lifestyle choices and behavioural norms.
4   . . . materials and processes.
5   . . . the relationships between its internal strengths and weaknesses and its external opportunities and threats.
6   . . . a company excels.
7   . . . external threats in terms of seriousness and occurrence probability.
8   . . . external opportunities in terms of attractiveness and success probability.
9   . . . evaluate a company's marketing objectives, policies and procedures as these relate to environmental influences and trends.
10   . . . the marketing performance of a company.
11   False
12   True
13   False
14   False
15   False

Chapter 4

1   . . . products, brand image, and general reputation.
2   . . . promote a company or its products.
3   . . . long-term relationships of mutual profitability.
4   . . . the brand, the company and the retail outlet.
5   . . . suspect, prospect, customer, client and advocate.
6   . . . build a positive company image in the local environment.
7   . . . the needs of the physical and social environment.
8   . . . natural resources should not be consumed at a greater rate than they can be replenished.
9   . . . satisfaction of customer needs, safety, social acceptability and sustainability.
10   . . . socio-environmental needs.
11   False
12   True
13   False
14   True
15   False

Chapter 5

1 ... intangibility, inseparability, perishability and variability.
2 ... the quality of a service depends on the personnel who deliver it.
3 ... aspects in the physical environment.
4 ... deliver the service dependably, accurately and consistently.
5 ... deliver the service promptly and helpfully.
6 ... deliver the service in a way that makes customers confident.
7 ... deliver the service in a way that shows understanding of individual customer needs.
8 ... their purpose is not primarily commercial.
9 ... providing a service which stands between the vulnerable and market forces.
10 ... rehabilitating vulnerable people.
11 False
12 True
13 True
14 True
15 True

Chapter 6

1 ... the right to safety, the right to be informed, the right to choose, and the right to be heard.
2 ... the physical environment or the long-term interests of consumers themselves.
3 ... the social and moral standards which are acceptable to a given society.
4 ... they are the work of a single company.
5 ... demonstrate that it has an effective, documented system for managing and developing its quality assurance.
6 ... the Independent Television Commission.
7 ... the Broadcast Advertising Clearance Centre.
8 ... Advertising Standards Authority.
9 ... Advertising Standards Authority.
10 ... Direct Marketing Association.
11 True
12 False
13 False
14 True
15 False

Chapter 7

1 ... an estimation of how many buyers there are in a total market.
2 ... how quickly market size will expand to reach its estimated potential.
3 ... market growth and market share.
4 ... market attractiveness and business strengths.

5 ... the generic product, the expected product, the augmented product and the potential product.

6 ... cost leadership, differentiation and focus.

7 ... attacking a competitor just before it launches an attack of its own.

8 ... wants to increase its market share by following an aggressive marketing strategy.

9 ... reduce a competitor's ability to defend itself.

10 ... companies are offering similar products to the same people.

11 True

12 True

13 False

14 False

15 False

Chapter 8

1 ... descriptive, strategic and operational.

2 ... was originally collected for another purpose, but which can be adapted for use by a marketing department.

3 ... they may deal in aggregates of data which are too broad to be of much use to the narrower interests of individual companies.

4 ... the processing of internal data from other departments within the company, as a means of recording company activity.

5 ... research carried out for a specific purpose and formally presented in a report.

6 ... carried out on a regular basis and is used to assist routine decision-making.

7 ... information expressed in numerical form.

8 ... not expressed in numerical form.

9 ... new product screening and test marketing.

10 ... market forecasts and sales forecasts.

11 False

12 True

13 False

14 True

15 False

Chapter 9

1 ... is designed to establish a causal relationship between two or more factors.

2 ... designing an experiment in the normal environment which is truly scientific.

3 ... can be representative of the consumer population as a whole.

4 ... a list of everyone in a given population.

5 ... known population.

6 ... approach a predetermined number of people.

7 . . . the respondent's answer is limited to 'Yes', 'No', or 'Don't know'.

8 . . . the respondent must select between several possible answers.

9 . . . rate how strongly they agree or disagree with a statement.

10 . . . direction and intensity of a respondent's knowledge or beliefs about a topic.

11 False

12 True

13 False

14 False

15 True

Chapter 10

1 . . . to give a visual sense of how each part compares to the others within a whole.

2 . . . central tendency.

3 . . . adding together the values in a list and then dividing by the number of items in the list.

4 . . . it can give a distorting impression if some values in a list are very high or very low.

5 . . . frequently-occurring value in a series.

6 . . . occurring in the middle of a series arranged in numerical order.

7 . . . discovering patterns in a company's sales volume over a given time.

8 . . . the smoothing process can hide the occurrence of new trends.

9 . . . regression line.

10 . . . zero correlation.

11 False

12 False

13 True

14 True

15 True

Chapter 11

1 . . . make the analysis of economic activity easier.

2 . . . the interaction of supply and demand.

3 . . . the quantity of a product or service demanded at a certain price.

4 . . . the lower the price, the greater the quantity that will be demanded.

5 . . . the higher the price, the greater the quantity that will be supplied.

6 . . . equilibrium price.

7 . . . the responsiveness of demand to changes in the price of a product or service.

8 . . . the responsiveness of supply to changes in the price of a product or service.

9 . . . theoretical combination of all the individual demand schedules for a product or service.

10 . . . rise in the short term.
11 False
12 True
13 True
14 False
15 False

Chapter 12

1 . . . the interaction of supply and demand.
2 . . . buyers are not in close contact with each other, and purchase decisions are frequently made on the basis of non-price considerations.
3 . . . perfectly elastic (horizontal).
4 . . . the total industry.
5 . . . the use of advertising and promotion to attract new customers to a company and existing customers away from competitors.
6 . . . dominated by a small number of suppliers.
7 . . . a company with many customers can make products more cheaply than smaller competitors through the use of automated production processes.
8 . . . a company with many customers can develop new products more cheaply than competitors because the fixed costs of new product development are spread over greater sales.
9 . . . all the suppliers in an industry agree to limit their output to the level that maximises their joint profits.
10 . . . oligopolies.
11 True
12 False
13 True
14 False
15 False

Chapter 13

1 . . . market structure, the way companies approach their customers, and the buying process.
2 . . . goods are purchased which will either be used to make products or be sold to customers.
3 . . . goods and services are purchased by distributors for resale to consumers.
4 . . . decision-making unit or buying centre.
5 . . . the company has no previous experience of the product or supplier.
6 . . . the company has some experience of the product or supplier, but some variable has changed.
7 . . . the company makes a routine re-ordering decision.
8 . . . the desire for rational outcomes influences purchase behaviour.
9 . . . non-task-related outcomes for individuals participating in the purchase process.

10 . . . psychological factors, decision-making and situational factors.
11 False
12 False
13 True
14 False
15 True

Chapter 14

1 . . . ad hoc judgements or an intuitive feel about the future.
2 . . . senior management.
3 . . . set targets and dates by which certain objectives should have been reached.
4 . . . the company's external and internal environments.
5 . . . how objectives will be reached.
6 . . . achieve marketing strategies.
7 . . . growth strategies.
8 . . . assess the performance of marketing activities.
9 . . . assess the extent to which a company has achieved planned sales levels.
10 . . . gauge the efficiency of marketing activities.
11 True
12 False
13 False
14 True
15 True

Chapter 15

1 . . . that each segment is identifiable, quantifiable, accessible and relevant.
2 . . . identifying groups of customers with different needs.
3 . . . dividing the market by reference to demographic factors.
4 . . . changing family structures and the changing role of women in the economy.
5 . . . segments the market according to various stages in family development.
6 . . . certain types of neighbourhood contain groups with similar demographic and social characteristics.
7 . . . regional studies.
8 . . . personality traits.
9 . . . inner-directed, outer-directed and sustenance-driven groups.
10 . . . criteria by which a consumer evaluates a product or service.
11 True
12 False
13 False
14 False
15 False

Chapter 16

1 . . . PEST factors.
2 . . . taxes on products crossing a national frontier.
3 . . . any form of government action designed to restrict imports.
4 . . . there is a high concentration on agriculture, and most output is consumed by the domestic market.
5 . . . there exists a wealth of raw materials which are exported.
6 . . . manufacturing accounts for 10–20 per cent of the country's gross national product.
7 . . . selected raw materials are imported and manufactured goods are exported.
8 . . . the short and long terms.
9 . . . characteristics which are perceived as disadvantageous.
10 . . . limited investment.
11 False
12 True
13 False
14 True
15 False

Glossary of terms

Ad hoc research – research carried out for a specific purpose

Agent – a marketing intermediary who does not take title to goods

Attitudes – favourable or unfavourable views of a company or product

Brand – a product which has received some form of identification which makes it immediately recognisable to customers

Buyer behaviour – analysis of the way customers behave

Buying centre – the group of people involved in making a company purchase decision

Cartel – an agreement between companies to act in concert, as if they were one seller

Cluster sampling – method of sampling in which the researcher approaches everyone in a defined area who has certain characteristics

Consumer – the final user of a product

Consumer goods – products marketed to individuals rather than organisations

Consumerism – partnership between pressure groups, consumer associations and governments to protect consumer interests

Consumer panel – a semi-permanent group of consumers who agree to record data in a diary

Continuous research – research carried out on a regular basis, which is used to support routine decision-making

Convenience goods – consumer products of low value which are purchased habitually or impulsively

Corporate objectives – statements about company purposes, with the dates by when targets should have been met

Cultural values – expression of a society's fundamental beliefs, attitudes, values, lifestyle choices and behavioural norms

Decider – person in a company with formal responsibility for taking purchase decisions

Decision-making unit – the group of people involved in making a company purchase decision

Demand – the quantity of a product or service that customers will be willing to buy at different prices

Demographics – the study of population changes

Descriptive research – research carried out into how something is operating

Desk research – research based on existing information sources

Disposable income – the income available to a household after tax payments have been made

Distribution channels – routes by which products are transferred to customers

Distributor – a marketing intermediary which distributes products

Elasticity – a measure of how much customer demand or supply changes relatively to changes in price

Entry barrier – any naturally-occurring or company-created barrier which inhibits the entry of new companies to an industry

Equilibrium quantity – the amount of a product or service that is bought and sold at the equilibrium price

Exclusive distribution – strategy designed to restrict the number of retail outlets for a product

Experiment – research method designed to establish causal relationship between two or more variables

Exploratory research – research carried out to gain initial insights into a situation, rather than to reach conclusions

Field research – the gathering of primary data for research

Gatekeeper – person in a company who controls the flow of information to and from members of the buying centre

Gross domestic product – the value of total output produced over a given period

Industrial goods – products needed by organisations

Influencer – anyone who influences a company purchase decision directly or indirectly

Intensive distribution – strategy designed to make a product available in the maximum number of retail outlets

Interest group – any group with an actual or potential interest in, or impact on, a company's ability to achieve its objectives

Intermediary – a person or organisation involved in moving products from manufacturers to end-users

Likert scale – a scale which allows respondents to record how strongly they agree or disagree with statements

Macro-environment – a company's external environment

Market development – one of the four strategies identified by I Ansoff

Market penetration – one of the four strategies identified by I Ansoff

Market research – research into any aspect of a company's markets

Market share – sales of a specific product compared with sales in the whole market, measurable by value or volume

Marketing audit – an examination of a company's external and internal environments

Marketing concept – the philosophy that company profitability comes from the successful identification and satisfaction of customer needs

Marketing mix – elements of marketing which come under the control of a company and are usually defined as product, price, promotion and place, although other elements such as people are sometimes added

Marketing planning – analysis of a company's internal and external environments in order to formulate objectives and strategies

Marketing research – the systematic gathering, recording and analysing of data about problems relating to the marketing of goods or services

Marketing strategy – statements of what is to be achieved, derived from corporate objectives

Mission statement – a senior-management decision about a company's current and future purposes, expressed in general terms

Modified re-buy – a purchase situation in which a company has some experience of the product or supplier, but some purchase factors are new

Monopoly – a market structure in which the output of an entire industry is controlled by one organisation

Motivational research – a qualitative technique used to investigate the hidden motives behind customer behaviour

Multistage sampling – a sampling technique designed to reduce the costs of a survey by obtaining a manageable sample

Needs – fundamental influences which drive human behaviour

New buy – a purchase situation in which the company has no previous knowledge of the product or supplier

Niche marketing – a marketing strategy which consists of focusing on highly specialised marketing segments

Non-profit organisation – organisation which seeks non-commercial responses from its markets

Observation – a research method used for investigating behaviour patterns

Oligopoly – a market structure in which sellers are very concentrated

Perfect competition – a market structure in which there are many sellers of an undifferentiated product

Personal interview – a research method in which respondents are interviewed by the researcher

PEST factors – the political, economic, socio-cultural and technological factors in a company's macro-environment

Place – one of the elements of the marketing mix

Postal survey – survey technique in which respondents are contacted through the post

Price – one of the elements of the marketing mix

Primary data – data from field research

Product – one of the elements of the marketing mix

Product life-cycle – stages of product development: introduction, growth, maturity, decline

Product line – related products made by the same company

Production orientation – the belief that company profitability comes from combining product quality with efficient production processes

Promotion – one of the elements of the marketing mix

Public relations – the deliberate, planned and sustained effort to establish and maintain mutual understanding between an organisation and its publics

Pull strategy – promotional strategy designed to encourage consumer demand for a product

Push strategy – promotional strategy designed to encourage intermediaries to promote a product to consumers

Qualitative research – research which is not expressed in numerical form

Quantitative research – research which is expressed in numerical form

Questionnaire – used to obtain information about a range of topics such as consumer habits, opinions, knowledge, attitudes, motivations or lifestyles

Quota sampling – sampling technique in which the researcher selects a predetermined number of people according to specified characteristics

Random sampling – sampling technique in which all members of the sampling frame have an equal chance of being included

Respondent – someone participating in a market research survey

Sales orientation – the belief that company profitability comes from effective selling

Sampling frame – a list of everyone in a given population

Secondary data – data which exists prior to a research project beginning

Selective distribution – strategy designed to ensure that a product is sold only through profitable or reputable outlets

Shopping goods – consumer products which are purchased after some thought

Skimming – a pricing strategy consisting of offering a product at a high price to capture specific market segments, and then dropping the price to appeal to wider segments

Societal marketing – the view that companies should examine how their marketing activities affect the social, business and physical environment

Speciality goods – consumer products about which the consumer has some knowledge

Straight re-buy – routine company purchase situation

Strategy – statement of how corporate objectives are to be reached

Supply – the quantity of a product or service that suppliers will be willing to put on the market at different prices

Systematic sampling – sampling technique in which a sample is obtained by dividing the number of people in a frame by the number of people to be sampled

SWOT analysis – examination of a company's internal strengths and weaknesses and external opportunities and threats

Tactics – specific action plans designed to achieve marketing strategies

Test marketing – technique for determining whether a new product is likely to perform well

Vertical marketing system – the co-ordination of distribution channels under the leadership of one channel member

Wants – the desire for specific needs-satisfiers

◆ Further reading

Adcock, D. *et al, Marketing Principles and Practice*, Pitman Publishing, 1993

Aguilar, F, *Scanning the Business Environment*, Macmillan, 1967

Ansoff, I, *Implementing Strategic Management*, Prentice-Hall, 1984

Ansoff, I, *Corporate Strategy*, Revised edn, Penguin, 1989

Bradley, F, *Marketing Management: providing, communicating and delivering value*, Prentice-Hall, 1995

Butler, J, *People and Organisations*, Oxford Business Publishing, 1991

Butler, J, *Marketing*, Oxford Business Publishing, 1991

Chisnall, P, *Strategic Industrial Marketing*, Prentice-Hall, 1985

Drucker, P, *The Practice of Management*, Pan, 1968

Jain, S, *Marketing Planning and Strategy*, 2nd edn, South-Western Publishing Company, 1985

Kotler, P, *Marketing Management*, 4th edn, Prentice-Hall, 1980

Kotler, P, *Marketing Management, Analysis, Planning, Implementation and Control*, 7th edn, Prentice-Hall, 1991

Kotler, P, and Singh, R, 'Marketing Warfare', *Journal of Business Strategy*, Winter 1981

Lancaster, G, and Massingham, L, *Marketing Management*, McGraw-Hill, 1993

Lancaster, G, and Massingham, L, *Essentials of Marketing*, 2nd edn, McGraw-Hill, 1993

Levitt, T, 'Marketing Myopia', *Harvard Business Review*, 1960

Levitt, T, *The Marketing Imagination*, Free Press, 1983

Lipsey, R, and Chrystal, K, *An Introduction to Positive Economics*, 8th edn, Oxford University Press, 1995

MacDonald, M, *Marketing Plans – and How to Use Them*, 2nd edn, Heinemann, 1989

Maslow, D, *Motivation and Personality*, Harper & Row, 1954

Packard, V, *The Waste Makers*, Penguin, 1960

Peattie, K, *Green Marketing*, Pitman Publishing, 1992

Peters, T, *Thriving on Chaos*, Macmillan, 1988

Porter, M, *Competitive Strategy: techniques for analysing industries and competitors*, Free Press, 1980

Porter, M, *Competitive Advantage: creating and sustaining superior performance*, Free Press, 1985

Robinson, P, Faris, C, and Wind, Y, *Industrial Buying and Creative Marketing*, Allyn and Bacon, 1967

Sheth, J, 'A Model of Industrial Buyer Behaviour', *Journal of Marketing*, 37, No. 4, October, 1973

Webster, F, and Wind, Y, *Organisational Buyer Behaviour*, Prentice-Hall, 1972

Index